AF568145

MILITARY CONVERSION

Impact on Science and Technology

MILITARY CONVERSION

Impact on Science and Technology

Editor

Dr. Digumarti Bhaskara Rao

Secretary

Academy of Communication Culture
Education Science and Service
1-22-10 Srinivasa Nagar
Guntur-522006 A.P.
India

2003

DISCOVERY PUBLISHING HOUSE
NEW DELHI-110002

First Published-2003

ISBN 81-7141-643-8

Published by

DISCOVERY PUBLISHING HOUSE
4831/24, Ansari Road, Prahlad Street,
Darya Ganj, New Delhi-110002 (India)
Phone: 3279245 • Fax: 91-11-3253475
E-mail:dphtemp@indiatimes.com

Printed at: Tarun Offset Printers, Delhi

Preface

The concept of establishing global peace is dramatically changing the functions of military industry. Many changes are occuring in this industry which have a bearing on science and technology. The articles presented in this book are dealing with the impact of military conversion on science and technology.

The editor is grateful to Prof. Pierre Lasserre, Director, UNESCO, Venice for giving permission to reproduce articles from the Proceedings of the International Round Table on Military Conversion and Science. He is thankful to Dr. Rosanna Santesso, UNESCO Venice office for her kind co-operation.

Digumarti B. Rao

Contents

CONTRIBUTORS

Airaghi Angelo

Senior Vice-President Finmeccanica SPA Viale Maresciallo Pilsudsky 92 Rome 00197, Italy.

Angell Ian

London School of Economic Houghton Street London WC2A 2AE, United Kingdom.

Biggin Susan

Consultant UNESCO-ROSTE Via Redipuglia 41 Ronchi dei Legionari-Gorizia 34077, Italy.

Borisov Boris

First Councillor Permanent Delegation of Russian Federation to UNESCO Paris 75016, France.

Borovik Sergei

Councillor Ministry of Foreign Affairs Mykhaylivska Square 1 Kiev 252018, Ukraine.

Caraça João

Director, Science Department Calouste Gulbenkian Foundation Avenida Berna 56-5a Lisbon 1093, Portugal.

Corsi Carlo

General Director Roma Ricerche Consorzio Roma Ricerche Alenia Finmeccanica Via Orazio Raimondo 8 Rome 00173, Italy.

Farinelli Fulvia

Research Assistant CNR Commission For Technological Research ENEA Dipartmento Innovazione ENEA INN-VALUS CNR Piazzale Aldo Moro-Rome 00100, Italy.

Kouzminov Vladimir

Chief, UNESCO-ROSTE Regional Office for Science and Technology for Europe 1262/A Dorsoduro-Venice 30123, Italy.

Macioti Manfredo

Founder Member Senior Experts Club Rue Guillaume Stocy 16 Brussels 1050, Belgium.

Magnaval Robert

European Union DG XII A-1 SDME 1.44 Rue de la Loi 200-Brussels 1049, Belgium.

Menano Horácio

Director Calouste Gulbenkian Foundation Rua Da Quinta Grande 6-Apartado 14 Oeiras 2781-Lisbon, Portugal.

Montanarelli Nicholas

Consultant Technology Reinvestment Project Department of Defense ARPA/TRP N. Fairfax Drive 3701 Arlington-Virginia 22203 United States of America.

Proctor John

Secretary General World Academy of Art and Science 308 East Street NE Vienna 22180, Virginia United States of America.

Shpak Anatolij

Chief Scientific Secretary Academy of Sciences of Ukraine 54 ul. Vladimirskaya Kiev 252601, Ukraine Stach Stanislav Scientific Worker Institute for Operational Art Research Ministry of Defence Branicke nam 2 14711 Prague 4, Czech Republic.

Traballesi Alberto

Deputy Chief Office for the Coordination of the Production of Armament Materials Presidency of the Ministers Council UCPMA Via Barberini 47-Rome 00187, Italy.

Zaleski Pierre

Member Board of Directors Moscow International Energy Club General Delegate CGEMP Paris Dauphine University Place du Marechal de Lattre de Tassigny 75775 Paris 16, France.

1

Military Conversion and Science

Introduction

The dramatic and far-reaching socio-economic and political changes in Central and Eastern Europe that began in the late 80's have prepared the ground for the establishment of global peace. Mankind had already been expecting the arrival of a widespread peace for half a century, and many societies widely believed that many vital but still open issues that threatened the globe's natural harmony could at last be settled.

As a result, "peace building" and "peace keeping" have become key words in our vocabularies, not only through our expectations of peace, but most particularly because peace has become a reality of our days, one that our offspring should enjoy.

The end of the Cold War and the dissolution of the superpower blocs has changed the role of international institutions, first and foremost that of the United Nations and its specialized agencies in their peace-building and peace-keeping missions. Today more than ever, new peace-building structures are needed to facilitate the transition from a culture of war to a culture of peace. Enormous opportunities for the socio-economic development of mankind have opened up, on the basis of the "peace dividend" resulting from the recent decline in global military spending.

UNESCO has always undertaken long-term actions to build the foundations of peace through education, science and culture, and communication and social sciences. These activities lie within the framework of one of the basic provisions recorded in UNESCO's Constitution by the organization's founders, which in particular declares that: "peace based exclusively upon the political and economic arrangements of governments would not be a peace which could secure the unanimous, lasting and sincere support of the world, and that the peace must therefore be founded, if it is not to fail, upon the intellectual and moral solidarity of mankind".

In response to the challenge of peace-building contained in the UN Secretary-General's Agenda for Peace, UNESCO has assumed a new and dynamic role, aimed at encouraging and reinforcing culture of peace in post-conflict, and especially pre-conflict situations. This is why UNESCO has launched its culture of peace programme. A culture of peace is the process of building trust and co-operation between peoples. Its means learning to use words instead of weapons to resolve conflicts It means fighting hunger and social injustice rather than each other. It means governments spending their resources on social programmes, not armies.

Of course, this is not an easy task for people and for organizations involved in the culture of peace process, especially at this initial phase.

Within this process, science, a unique phenomenon of mankind and integral part of his culture, occupies a special, very delicate position since has been one of the major contributors to the creation of giant war arsenals worldwide. During the Cold War period, many countries made intense use of both fundamental and applied science for military research and development, for creating sophisticated arms for mass-killing. Enormous capital investment have been made to date in building research centres and production capacities for this purpose. Into this military-oriented R&D effort were poured the best brains of almost all industrially developed countries: in consequence, the military-industrial complex is a possession of high intellectual potential which can and should be used for resolving the world community's most urgent problems.

The process of military conversion or defence conversion was begun on the basis of historical agreements between superpowers to drastically reduce their military arsenals and consequently military-oriented research and arms production.

The first roots of military conversion were put down a few years ago in the USA and the Russian Federation, followed soon after by other nations. Unfortunately, it was discovered that this process needs at least initially considerable capital investment in order to convert military R&D to civilian needs.

Morever, it was discovered that in some countries this process is accompanied by new phenomena capable of causing additional tensions and instability within and external to the contries concerned.

One such is the "brain drain": it has been studied and discussed in detail at a number of international meetings held by different international organizations including UNESCO-ROSTE.

The problems of military conversion and their interaction with science, probably one of the most fragile components of the military-industrial complex, constitute a uniting global issue for learned societies, academies and organizations supporting and advancing basic research and technological development.

Many questions then arise. Just who should support science in this transitional period, in what way, how should the transformation be managed to be most effective, to avoid loss of intellectual potential at national and international level; how can defence-research science be redirected towards basic and vitally important problems such as environmental protection, human health, food production, and so on, how should this branch of science contribute to the peace-building and peace-keeping process throughout the world? These and other issues need close analysis, not least in order to be prepared for some of the consequences that can flare up and are hard to predict, even at this current stage of socio-economic development.

The International Round Table on Military Conversion and Science was convened in an attempt to clarify just such issues.

Military Conversion

Military conversion, or defence conversion, is taken to mean the management of change in the military and its supporting industrial base that has resulted from the problems in the current global political and economic climate. Today's military systems are extremely complex and have become too expensive to maintain: as a response, governments worldwide envisage a conversion to simplified and cheaper systems. But in all systemic environments, the switching from one stable state to another will require the consumption of energy. With social systems, this means the expenditure of effort and funding. Piecemeal reduction of a stable but undesirable system always results in chaos, and not stability. In this context, in the absence of specific defence conversion, military capability disintegration will ensue. In fact, what we are seeing at the moment is military contraction and not military conversion. We must consider the long-term vulnerability that is a consequence of such action.

There are three major inter-related aspects to be dealt with: (i) the maintaining of a "minimum" state-of-the-art capability (military readiness to deal with a politically chosen part of the threat spectrum which must be preserved); (ii) the doing away with redundant capabilities and capacities; and (iii) absorption of products and personnel into the general economy.

Issues to examine include science and technology, human resources dislocations, incentive strategies, socio-economic phenomena such as brain drain, the transformation of educational and scientific institutions and of culture in general. The machinery of conversion is to be driven in parallel with the new culture of peace being promoted by UNESCO.

The process of military conversion has the by-product of unemployable or unfunded and underfunded military personnel and of scientists and technologists. Strategically driven military conversion aims to minimise waste of intellectual resources and maximise the exploitation of existing technologies for civilian use.

While global war is now less likely, regional threat to security has increased and the probability of local, tactical wars remains unchanged or even increased by the need of ethnic and religious groups for self-protection. The UNESCO Culture of Peace Programme aims to use transdisciplinary education to teach tolerance, overcoming resistance to change, and encouraging openness to the idea of learning to learn. Increased worldwide employment of women in science and their greater role in peacekeeping policy generation, implementation and evaluation, could lead to a softening of masculine, aggressive decision-making. A great deal of thought must be given to the effects of the change on future generations. We are already experiencing a disillusionment with science among school children who perceive little reward for the years of effort needed to become qualified scientists. It is, nevertheless, clear that science is one of the most important aspects of society, and should be given stronger promotion and made more accessible to non-scientists.

Science

Within the military-industrial complex is a high proportion of the world's science and scientists. Conversion will therefore mean a new outlook for science itself as well as the absorption and redeployment of scientists. In this new science, there will be reduced R&D expenditure, which prompts the question of who is to pay for basic science.

Cost

High capital investment is required, at least in the short term, to create an efficient and stable long-term solution. It will be at least as costly as maintaining the status quo.

A few governments may benefit from military conversion by investing in dual-use technologies. In addition, some cost benefits may arise from international agreements or exchanges of commodities or capabilities.

On the whole, though, there will be no profit from military conversion itself. The anticipated benefits of redirecting military budgets into welfare are as much a myth as the peace dividend.

Timing

Medium- to long-term planning is essential not only for decision-making processes but also bearing in mind the inertia of industry. It must be recognised that there are no "quick fixes" to military conversion - 20 years of patient effort may be needed for conversion to the civilian sphere, and even then the likelihood of success is uncertain. Constant monitoring should be written into any proposals, for measuring the overall success of conversion and non-conversion. Through time, it must be remembered that defence conversion is strongly context-dependent.

Legislation

New legislation coupled with normative economic measures are required by individual nation states to enable them to meet their individual requirement for military conversion and science preservation, including safeguards for the protection of new technologies and attendant intellectual property rights.

Personnel and Brain Drain

Care must be taken to absorb discharged military and civilian personnel employed by government to minimise potential conflicts within the general employment market. Attention must be given to maintaining jobs for the employable and incentives for retaining should be established. The talented scientists should not be left adrift in the wrong environment or given cause to seek satisfaction or remuneration in undesirable situations, or to be lured away from science into more remunerative employment in the business world.

Types of Conversion

Military establishments should be involved. While some three-quarters of military structures can convert easily (buildings, some jobs, some equipment), the rest (laboratories and the brains of some types of science) will not convert either quickly or cheaply.

Care must be taken with the speed and degree of military conversion, achieving as nearly as possible as workable balance between the military-industrial complex and the rest of the civilian economy. Unrealistic expectations could destroy the military industrial base and produce very costly dislocation in civilian industries. This suggests that regional, continental and international joint ventures or consortia could produce less costly, more sustainable solutions.

MILITARY CONVERSION: IMPACT ON SCIENCE AND TECHNOLOGY

2

"It was the best of times, it was the worst of times"

Ian Angell

Introduction

"It was the best of times, it was the worst of times, it was the age of wisdom, it was the age of foolishness, it was the epoch of belief, it was the epoch of incredulity, it was the season of Light, it was the season of Darkness, it was the spring of hope, it was the winter of despair, we had everything before us, we had nothing before us, we were all going direct to Heaven, we were all going direct the other way".

The first words of *A Tale of Two Cities*, used by Charles Dickens to describe the French Revolution, ring hauntingly true today. For we are on the verge of another revolution, a new social and economic reality, perched on the "Edge of Chaos" - an Information Revolution that is taking us out of the Machine Age, into... who knows what.

This "Information Age" (see Daniel Bell [1]) will be just as significant as those of the Industrial Revolution. The very natures of work, of society, and even of capitalism itself, are mutating. These mutations are confronting each other in the political power vacuum left by the fall of communism, and the increasing impotence of liberal democracy when facing both the mass unemployment of its citizens, and the likely mass migration of the exploding population of the Third World (95% of the world's population increase is in developing countries: see Kennedy [2]).

The End of History?

Francis Fukuyama [3], in his book *The End of History and the Last Man,* claimed that liberal democracy had triumphed. Like Hegel and Marx before him, he saw the perfectibility of the political system, hence "the End of History". The Soviet "evil empire" had fallen with hardly a shot being fired; the Berlin Wall likewise. US President George Bush foresaw a democratic "New World Order" in the end of the Cold War - aimed to give the voters a nice warm glow? But it is a glow of wishful thinking, encapsulated in terms like the "peace dividend" and "human rights"; a glow that is merely an illusion that will be shattered before the global economic realities to come in "Information Age". The "peace dividend" already looks like a sick joke to the redundant of the world's defence industries; how long will it be before the notion of "human rights" is as outdated as the "Divine Right of Kings"?

These smug claims of a complete victory for enlightened liberal democracy sound singularly hollow before various military adventures in the Third World, the rabid nationalism of "ethnic cleansing", and hypocrisy of national boundaries slamming shut against the mass movement of populations. Perhaps the optimists are deluding themselves? Perhaps it is raw capitalism and not democracy that has prevailed? Perhaps today's fashionable version of democracy is the next to fall?

The world's media is speculating on a growing sense of global foreboding, uncertainty and gloom, bemoaning a worldwide crisis of confidence in social, political and economic institutions. The very past success of these institutions has made them degenerate, and has spawned systems of such complexity, that the old certainties are beginning to fail: *"nothing fails like success"* (Kenneth Boulding).

The New Barbarians

So is it the End of History? No! *"History is the natural selection of accidents"* (Trotsky) and our world is now full of accidents waiting to happen. *"Those who can't remember the past are condemned to repeat it"* (Santayana). Without a sense of the historic context of the present uncertainty, we will be unable to comprehend the forces of disorder that are undermining today's certainties.

Our present situation sounds hauntingly familiar. The more things change, the more they stay the same. In 358AD Rome, a long-standing civilization based on organizational skills, commerce and technology, confident in its superiority, fell to the barbarian, hordes that were once its servants. Rome didn't just disappear, choice fragments were looted and reformed into new orders. Today the socio-political order of our civilization is on the verge of collapse. What will happen to us, now it is our turn? The coming millennium will be a time of amazing opportunities, emerging through the heroic actions of individuals and organizations; heroic, that is, in the classical sense. These opportunists, who will loot our civilization, I have come to call "the new barbarians".

"Now there are coming new barbarians cynics experimenters conquerors union of spiritual superiority with well-being and an excess of strength.

I point to something new: certainly for such a democratic type there exists the danger of the barbarian, but one has looked for it only in the depths. There exists also another type of barbarian, who comes from the heights: a species of conquering and ruling natures in search of material to mould. Prometheus was this kind of barbarian."

(Friedrich Nietzsche [4])

But why now? Quite simply, today's new technologies have unleashed unstoppable economic forces which are empowering adolescent forms of new barbarism. The new barbarians are imaginative outsiders who know that there are enormous opportunities for those who have the vigour and vitality to break free of the limitations of boundaries drawn from the past, and who can create their own boundaries, their own future.

The "new barbarian" hypothesis is not in itself a specific predictor of things to come. It is an account of the societal mechanism that drives transition and that recurs throughout human history, but particularly during times of turmoil, complexity and uncertainty. A mechanism whereby opportunists sweep away old moribund institutions, not in anarchy and chaos, but with new ideas, new moralities and new power structures; subsequently laying the foundations for new institutions: the "New Order".

No Pride and no Shame

Democratic politicians are perpetually surprised by these amoral opportunists who profit from treading a different path. In vain, our "representatives" try to legislate against them, and they have often succeeded in the past (witness USA against

Leona Helmsley of *"only the little people pay taxes"* fame). But these politicians are just whistling in the wind of change (or should that be pissing into the wind?). Soon only the little people will pay taxes, the new barbarians will have a choice.

All the while, Western politicians are pandering to the masses by affecting the poses of CNN anchor-men (characterless good looks and perfect teeth), and espousing the fascism of political correctness. All the while they fail to see in it the excesses of a popular *"ideological thuggery"*; the hell of a collectivist heaven. But while the politicians are posing for the peasants, the new barbarians are carving out the New Order, as when money markets manipulate national currencies, and pour scorn on the pathetic pleas of finance ministers.

Impotent politicians worldwide (even Karl Marx anticipated politicians becoming ineffective, but for other reasons!) want to appear moral in their power broking. They seek the justification for their selfish actions in an infinitely flexible "international law". Yet they are thoroughly bewildered when the consequences of their actions finesse, even reverse, their best intentions.

But they should care? Politics has become a profession, and in these cynical and degenerate times politicians display no sense of pride and no sense of shame. More and more they are seen as self-seekers, losing all respect of those they represent. Nowadays, no-one believes them any more, or even cares. The latest "sleaze" scandals in Britain are not unexpected:
"giving money and power to government is like giving whiskey and car keys to teenage boys" (P.J. O'Rourke)
"when buying and selling are controlled by legislation, the first things to be bought and sold are legislators". (P.J. O'Rourke)
"Professional people have no cares
Whatever happens they get theirs" (Ogden Nash)

The Myth of Control

What is going on? How have the pathetic politicians lost control over the course of events? How is it that they stand before us with sham, bluster, superficiality and panic, while their old certainties are falling apart?

All around the globe there is a growing sense of unease, and undercurrent of uncertainty, a feeling that it is all running out of control. With louder and louder voices, politicians parade and preen, and dabble on the world stage. The press and media cynically report it; they themselves now precipitate much that is news. Many business leaders are no better, as they perform the ritual incantations of market forces and pontificate about "Management of Change" and "Business Process Re-engineering". But it doesn't fool anybody. Their frantic search for a tidy and scientifically (= democratically) correct schema is just an admission that the "experts" don't know what to do. Their Myth of Control is laid bare. All around us the institutional procedures that have stood the test of decades, centuries even, are degenerating. The sight of world leaders in a frenzy of meddling, and Nero-like fiddling is most unedifying. The glue of the old order, hypocrisy, is now coming unstuck.

History in Reverse

As you have already gathered, I disagree totally with Fukuyama's claims that History is ending and that there are *"No barbarians at the gates"* (a chapter in his book). For fundamental in his updated historicism of Hegel and Mark, is a belief in the unhindered continuation of collectivism; the tribe, the state, the herd supreme. As you will also realize, I do not accept that the utopian ideology of modern-day liberal democracy has triumphed once and for all. Like Imperial Rome, all I see in the triumph of universal franchise is "bread and circuses" for the masses (entertainment/television, sport, pop music), the death-throws preceding decline and fall.

Fukuyama fails to see that democracy is itself barbarism, an old and now degenerate barbarism. The barbarism of the many against the few, barbarism become respectable through being the norm, but barbarism all the same, a barbarism whose time has come... and gone. *"A democracy cannot exist as a permanent form of government. It can only exist until a majority of voters discover that they can vote themselves largesse out of the public treasury"* (Alexander Tytler reported in [5]).

Make way for the new barbarians, the opportunists awaiting their chance to hijack the future, and form a new order. The seeds of this new order are already here, they have always been here, they have already germinated. But are they friend or foe? They are the individuals and transnational organizations and companies that hold no loyalties to the herd. They are the press barons, the market manipulators, international businessmen, international terrorists, drug barons, neo-colonialist non-governmental organizations, criminal organizations, rejuvenated forms of older religious and political fundamentalists, amoral individualists; they are the power brokers, now cut free from the constraints of national boundaries by the new communication technologies. They are the virile, vigorous and vital opportunists who will strike at the power base of impotent politicians, bewildered businessmen and all the other trivialisers of our Age - and their time is coming, for *"history is on their side"*.

The new barbarians are here, they have already breached the smug walls of liberal democracy. They are the very reason for the uncertainty of our time. But blinkered by a present obsessed with past certainties, their growth remains shrouded to all but the most perceptive. The coming millennium will finally bury the ideologies of the present century, the "century of the collective". The two hundred years of "social progress", instigated by the then-new barbarians of the French Revolution, are slowly being rolled back. History isn't ending, it is going into reverse (Baudrillard [6]).

Transition to a New Order

The drowning media are frantically clutching at straws. Many, if not most of today's commentators are deeply pessimistic, they see only chaos ahead. They see chaos because they are interpreting events in terms of the very control structures and institutions that are failing. They are reflecting an increasingly uncertain tomorrow in the distorting mirror of yesterday's defunct certainties. They want the world to be the way it ought to be.

The prevalent hope is that a flow tide of chaos can be turned back by re-imposing the old order, by reasserting strong social, political and economic control. Even though the times are changing, King Canute is alive and well, and has entered politics. His stance is a complete misunderstanding of the human condition. Control doesn't create order, just the opposite; order must be there first, and this order tolerates control. The pundits are confusing order with structure and stability; they are confusing cause and effect. Only by the concession of order, does the consequent control impose structure and stability. All order is transitory; order allows controls to work, and then order fails; consequently the certainty of control and structure collapses.

A new order is transparent to old perspectives; a new order can only be understood through the development of different ideas. *"The difficulty lies not in creating new ideas but in escaping from old ones"* (John Maynard Keynes).

The old controls and institutions are failing; uncertainty, as always, precedes the transition to a new order - and new controls. We live in a state of continuous and unremitting transition, it never goes away, it is only a matter of scale - sometimes that scale merits the label revolution. Will the future brand our present age as a time of revolution?

A New Philosophy

The Industrial Revolution seemed like chaos to those living through it. To old perspectives, any major transition to a new order seems like chaos; for the trend to a new order can only be recognized through the development of new and different ideas. *"When we lose the comfortable formulas that have hitherto been our guides among the complexities of existence... we feel like drowning in the ocean of facts until we find a new foothold or learn to swim"* (Werner Sombart, reported [5]).

So who will help us swim? Who will be the true voice of the new generation? Who will give us a philosophy to explain the new age? Who will be the new Karl Marx for the coming millennium? We won't have to wait. He was born one hundred and fifty years ago (15 October 1844); he died just before this present century, which he would have despised, had begun (25 August 1900). Friedrich Nietzsche has given us his Zarathustra [7] and his *"philosophy with a hammer"* in numerous books [4], [8].

To him the future is going to be brutal; a future born of conflict. A conflict that is mitigated to a certain extent by a predisposition towards human virtues. But virtues based on strength, not weakness. *"I have often laughed at the weaklings who thought themselves good because they had no claws"*. There has to be a disposition to confrontation - that even welcomes it. *"One is punished for being weak, not for being cruel"* (Baudelaire). Through conflict the new barbarians will be tempered in the flames of competition, and succeed. Their *"paradise lies in the shadow of swords"*. Now more than ever before, the state needs its military-industrial complex.

Nietzsche recognized that democracy is basically a single platform - that of the virtue of tribal moralities: back to "basic values", the *"morality of the herd"*, the "common good", power fixed in the tribe. But the new barbarians ignore tribal boundaries, tribal loyalties. The new barbarians see no particular virtue in the common good. To them the common good is not necessarily good, it is merely... common! They see modern-day democracy for what it is, a once-proud individualistic label that has been hijacked by collectivism. They know democracy in its present form will continue for the time being, but it will be of no consequence to them. Times of uncertainty call out for leadership; but not leadership that panders to the "greatest good" and to egalitarian ideals, for that is a formula for mediocrity. *"There is no justice in equality"*. To succeed, leadership must be strong in its striving - ruthless. New barbarians assert that healthy systems expel all poisons from within. *"Nature is not immoral when it has no pity for the degenerate"*.

"It was the best of times, it was the worst of times". We will be holding our discussion against the background of today's global degeneracy that I have described. Will we find *"the spring of hope"* or *"the winter of despair"*? You can guess what I believe. I am looking forward to hearing your opinions over the next two days.

REFERENCES

1. BELL D. (1976), *The Coming of the Post-Industrial Society: A Venture in Social Forecasting*, Basic Books, New York.
2. KENNEDY P. (1993), *Preparing for the Twenty-First Century*, Fontana, London.
3. FUKUYAMA F. (1992), *The End of History and the Last Man*, Penguin, London.
4. NIETZSCHE F. (1968), *Will to Power*, Vintage, New York.
5. CARR E.H. (1990), *What is History*, Penguin, London.
6. BAUDRILLARD J. (1994), *The Illusion of the End*, Polity Press, Cambridge
7. NIETZSCHE F. (1969), *Thus spoke Zarathustra*, Penguin, London.
8. NIETZSCHE F. (1990), *Beyond Good and Evil*, Penguin, London.

3

Trends in RD Expenditures in the Community: Diversification in the Civilian Field *

Robert Magnaval

The changes that have occurred in central and eastern Europe have drastically altered the perception of a global and immediate threat that previously existed in the West. This change is often traced back to the fall of the Berlin wall. In fact it was the Soviet US summit in Reykjavik in 1985 that set this process in motion. Western countries took advantage of the summit to cut their military budgets at a time when government finances were beginning to show serious deficits. The period from '90 to '92 witnessed an accelerating downward trend in the budgets of member states of the European Union. This reduction stabilized at around 3 to 4% and is set to continue until 1996. In the USA real defence expenditure is expected to drop by 45 to 50% from 1990 to the year 2000 (OTA 1993) and, according to estimates made by the European Research Institute on Peace and Security GRIP (1993), the ratio of military expenditure to GDP through the Community will fall from 3% in 1986 to 1.8% in 1996.

Since the end of confrontation between the two blocs, tensions have nevertheless not disappeared. There are plenty of examples of conflict due to fundamentalist pressures, fervent na-

---

* Review of the literature based on data published in the "European Report on Science and Technology Indicators" eds. U. Muldur & L. Soete, Office for Publications of the European Communities, Report EUR 15897, 1994, 338 p. and "L'industrie européenne de l'Armement: Recherche, Développement Technologique et Reconversion", STOA/GRIP Report, Ed. P. de Vestel European Parliament, 1993, 109 p.

tionalism and economic tensions but military intervention alone is no longer regarded as a course of action capable of solving these crises (SRI, 1994).

1. Reductions in Budgets and Changes in Employment

It is estimated that direct employment in the armaments industry amounted to 660,000 jobs in the Community in 1992. The rate of reduction in these jobs since 1984 has been twice as fast as the reduction in the turnover of the defence industry. On the basis of this data, two scenarios were predicted and described during a symposium organised by Science & Technology Options Assessment (STOA) in the European Parliament in 1993:

- One scenario assumes that the defence budgets of member states will fall from 117 billion ECU in 1992 to 103 billion ECU in 1996 (an annual drop of 3.2%) with exports stabilizing and the turnover of armaments firms dropping from 49 to 43 billion ECU with the loss of 145,000 jobs by 1996;
- The other scenario foresees these budgets falling twice as much accompanied by an annual reduction in exports of 5% which is the average rate observed since 1984 (Table 1). Job losses in manufacturing will amount to 220,000 jobs by 1996.

Cutbacks in civilian and military manpower in associated subcontracting activities and cuts in defence ministry personnel must be added to these figures. It is estimated that the number of jobs that will be lost every year over the next two years will be more than 100,000.

Two other factors help make diversification unavoidable:

- The opening up of defence markets with competitive tendering by several suppliers forces companies to alter their customs and practices to match those in the civilian field.
- As far as the drop in exports associated with reduced de-

fence efforts in developing countries and its consequences on industrial activity are concerned, the reader should refer to the data published by the Stockholm International Peace Research Institute (SIPRI) in 1993. It must not be overlooked that, between 1984 and 1991, exports from the European Union fell by 40% in volume and that the armaments industry in Europe is more heavily reliant on exports than is the US armaments industry.

2. Industrial Conversion and Diversification

The process of conversion due to the reduction in public funding mentioned earlier has been accompanied by restructuring of armed forces in Europe intended to enhance their mobility, speed of intervention, specialisation and multinational character. The main thrusts of this approach involve, in particular, aerial or space intelligence, communication networks, logistics and interoperability.

Many obstacles have been encountered in attempting to free up the necessary resources for these redefined needs. One of these is the inherent inertia of the military whose mode of operation and traditional missions do not naturally lend themselves to cooperation and exchanging information. Other problems are created by economic and social resistance in response to cutbacks in public expenditure whether they involve job losses or reduced purchasing of equipment (Table 1). Nevertheless, Europe is not completely inexperienced in matters of industrial restructuring. One could cite the case of the iron and steel industry which reduced its manpower by 52% from 1975 to 1990 at a rate comparable to that planned in defence industries over the ten years from 1986 to 1996. The defence industry has several trump cards it can play in order to cope with this sudden transformation. The geographical distribution of defence firms is more balanced than that of the iron and steel industry. Some firms are located in regions that have significant capacity to adapt. The widely varied qualifications of personnel create the option of transferring labour from the military to the civilian field, an option that more traditional sectors do not have.

Faced with this economic situation, companies have had to make choices. They have often increased the range of their multiple products. They have blended a specialisation strategy in the military sector (expanding niche market, export effort, cooperation between firms) with a passive (production cutback) or active retrenchment strategy (policy of acquiring stakes in civilian activities closely related to military activities (aerospace, car electronics, shipyards). Other firms have gradually withdrawn. Here too there are similarities and echoes of the process of transforming the economy from a war footing at the end of World War II, a task completed successfully within a few years. However, many companies involved in that process already had experience in the civilian field at the time whereas this does not apply to companies that are currently having to be converted. It is also clear that caution prevails: conversion in the strict sense of the word is rarely applicable, diversification is more frequently encountered. Regardless of the strategy adopted it is always confronted by an unfavourable general economic climate.

Such necessary adjustments are accompanied by intervention by government bodies. In Europe intervention is patterned on the measures taken as part of the restructuring of other sectors the iron and steel industry mentioned earlier is a good example. At the end of 1990 the Community launched the PERIFRA initiative backed by 90 million ECU; 58% of the funds supported projects linked to the reduction in military expenditure. In 1993 the KONVER programme was allocated 130 million ECU provided by the European Regional Development Fund (100 million) and the European Social Fund (30 million). In the future the KONVER II Community initiative will last several years and be allocated 500 million over the period 1994-

1997 (EC, 1994). In this regard, one should point out the weaknesses in statistical data making it possible to assess the local impact of reduced activity in employment areas, something that makes it difficult to target intervention and concentrate Community action. KONVER differs in many respects from the programme implemented in the USA. It involves a regional rather than an engineering conversion campaign. As far as the support provided is concerned, the pluriannual KONVER plan is equivalent to half the aid provided by the American Technology Reinvestment Project programme.

3. Technology Research and Development

Member states invested 11.3 billion ECU in research and development in 1990; these amounts are calculated on the basis of the expenditure earmarked in the national budgets. These data differ from those of the OECD by roughly 4% (Table 2). There are no precise details on R&D investment specific to companies which is estimated at approximately 2 billion ECU and mainly originates from French and British companies (GRIP, 1993). The distribution of research budgets between the various states revealed a wide variety of situations (Table 2). France and Great Britain are the European Economic Area (EEA) states most committed to military research effort, Germany, Spain, Italy and Sweden account for most of the remainder. Most military research is carried out within companies: 60% in the case of Great Britain and 52% in France (CREDIT, 1993). Table 3 summarises the data in Table 2 for the Big Three (Europe, USA, Japan) and shows that the American effort remains the biggest. Military research budgets in Japan and, to a lesser extent, in France are increasing and differ from the generally observed trend and, as is the case in the USA, this is explainable as stabilization after a sharp fall. Several reasons have been put forward to explain this development that has had little impact on research credits and sharp cuts in defence budgets (Table 1).

It is alleged that research capability is being preserved in order to multiply dual-use research and development lines with public support for research making it possible to accomplish the pilot phase (design of prototypes) without nevertheless financing subsequent production stages with a view to making savings. Major states are said to be carrying out an "upstream" technology watching brief.

One must nevertheless be cautious when interpreting the figures quoted for the defence industry because they do not necessarily correspond to research activities as defined by international bodies for civilian activities (CREDIT, 1993). One must also not overlook the fact that military research is generally scheduled over several years and, consequently, planned budgets and actual annual expenditure may differ significantly.

France and Great Britain, countries that are close to the American model, have an important share of DIRD that must be subtracted from normal mechanisms for directing and assessing research policy. The markets for which the results of such research are intended are often predetermined and have been protected for a long time.

The scheduling of this part of research corresponds to a linear representation of its role. Fundamental research, development and production are activities that are linked in a sequential and unambiguous manner. Comparative analysis of national systems for innovation shows that the weight of military research has also influenced, in these countries, the arrangements for defining the overall national research policy. Policies for missions with "targeted" or "enabling" programmes have been given preference rather than more horizontal actions (Nat. Inn. Systems, 1993).

In these countries, the relationship between science, political power and military research that had become clearly established before the second world war has persisted during subsequent years. For a long time it was taken for granted that military technology, which benefited from unstinting finance, was ahead of civilian research. A number of examples to the contrary slightly altered this view in the 80's but nowadays the crumbling of defence budgets only highlights such doubts. Statistics that record the economic spin-offs from military research are nevertheless rare. British consultants ACOST (1989) estimated the proportion of the military R&D budget that could have civilian applications at 20%. The demand for leading-edge technologies that meet the needs of a financially solvent civilian economy has now overtaken military demand. The process is being reversed to the extent that military applications may depend on technology innovations of civilian origin or developments for civilian or military use (dual technologies). The Industrial R&D Advisory Committee (IRDAC) emphasized the importance of efforts to adapt defence-linked research in the report that it submitted to the fourth Outline Programme (1994-1998) of the Community for technology research and development campaigns.

4. Coordination of Research and Development Efforts

Cooperation in matters of military research always involves tricky negotiations but it is necessary in Europe for at least two reasons. One reason is associated with the desire to avoid pointless duplication and the other reason is the interdependence of civilian and military R&D activities.

In the first matter, the European Independent Programme Group (EIPG) launched the European Cooperative Long Term Initiative in Defence (EUCLID) programme in 1988. This cooperation has now been entrusted to the Western European Armaments Group that reports to the UEO in 1993. Planned total financial backing for the EUCLID programme is 120 million ECU and roughly 50% of this budget has already been committed since the programme was launched. Italy is one of the most active partners (12% of resources). Despite this, cooperation is difficult to set up and contracts worth only 30 million ECU were awarded in 1993.

In the second matter, it has already been stated that the quality of technology performance in the civilian field rivals that in the defence sector. The boundary between military research and civilian research is tending to become blurred as the markets themselves open up and penetrate each other. Collaboration in defining research policies is inadequate. As the "Growth, Competitivity, Employment" White Paper (1993) states: "this weakness is apparent in each member state between military research and civilian research carried out within fairly impermeable institutional frameworks". One might add that the organisation of research departments in firms that have "dual" production also reflects this dichotomy.

Interdependence between civilian and military research raises the problem of coordinating the policies that sustain them. It is therefore not surprising that public intervention has been compelled to support the setting up of scientific and engineering networks that unite all those involved.

5. Cooperative Research, an Instrument for Diversification and Collaboration

Europe is in a good position to use all the resources offered by cooperative research in order to redirect and diversify the allocation of public funds in line with the needs of industry. Europe can draw on many national experiences in order to achieve this: Fraunhofer Gesellschaft, LINK programme, community programmes: ESPRIT, RACE, BRITE-EURAM or European programmes: European Space Agency. Europe has also perceived the full benefit that it can obtain from such a mechanism. Note that the EUREKA civilian programme was launched in Europe in response to the American Strategic Defense Initiative in 1985.

Ten years of experience in matters of cooperative research demonstrate the richness of interaction between university and industrial research. This cooperation multiplies the economic effects anticipated by industry taken individually by a factor or 2 (EC, 1994).

DIRECT AND INDIRECT ECONOMIC EFFECTS OF COMMUNITY SUPPORT TO INDUSTRIAL TECHNOLOGY AND MATERIAL RESEARCH

CONSORTIA WITH ACADEMIC PARTNERS (1)
29 ECU

COMMUNITY RTD SUPPORT
1 ECU

CONSORTIA WITHOUT (1)
14 ECU

(1) BASED ON AN ASSESSMENT OF THE BRITE EURAM EC PROGRAMME CONDUCTED BY BETA, UNIV. STRASBOURG (1993).

In the current phase of bringing together military and civilian research, this interactive mechanism will, by its very nature, have an incentivising role in avoiding pointless duplication by encouraging flexibility and collaboration, if necessary, in a difficult budgetary context. The new US administration also has a global approach to national security questions that integrates technological development, economic performance and defence questions.

The benefits of the link between the Pentagon and US microelectronics firms in the SEMATECH consortium have encouraged those in charge to promote more interventionist policies. The ARPA agency coordinates the development of dual-use technologies as part of the Technology Reinvestment Project mentioned under heading 2. The US administration is now keen to free federal laboratories from their dependence on the Department of Energy (DOE) and the Department of Defense (DOD). This implies a modification of US legislation: the Federal Technology Transfer Act of 1986 and National Competitiveness Technology Transfer Act of 1989 (NSF, 1993). The USA has used the mechanisms provided by cooperative research in order to facilitate the transfer of results of research as well as that of the know-how of researchers. One of the instruments used by all US federal agencies consists of Cooperative Research and Development Agreements (CRADAs). The number of these agreements grew from 33 in 1987 to 1175 in 1992, all federal agencies included. The extension of CRADA agreements to national laboratories dependent on the DOE defence programme required long negotiations that lasted from 9 to 24 months before they could be implemented. There were only 15 agreements in 1991 as opposed to 382 in early 1993 (OTA, 1993) but the financial limits remain modest: less than 300 million ECU. Questions of confidentiality, copyright, national preference and legal responsibility linked to commercial exploitation have been systematized, but not without some difficulty. 40 years of close links between major armament companies and the DOD are not easy to reorganise. Many observers still have reservations regarding the outcome of this policy (B. Berkowitz, 1994).

At the Community level, the French General Delegation for Armement (DGA) has recently analysed the capacity of the Community's fourth framework programme (1994-1998) to facilitate the diversification strategy of industry. DGA estimates that one third of the activities of the different research and technological development activities proposed for the period (1994-1998) might be of interest for concerned industries or agencies. It corresponds to 3.6 million ECU out of the overall amount of 12.3 billion for that period.

Fourth Framework Programme (1994-1998)	Total amount Millions ECU	Dual use/ diversific. (1) %	Partial amount diversific.
Telematics	843	20%	168
Communication technologies	630	57%	360
Information technologies	1932	84%	1622
Industrial technologies and materials technologies	1707	30%	512
Standardization, measurement and testing	288	10%	28
Environment and climate	852	11%	93
Marine sciences and technologies	228		
Biotechnology	552		
Biomedicine and health	336	50%	168
Agriculture and fisheries (including agro-industry, food technologies, forestry, aquaculture and rural development)	684	0%	0
Non-nuclear energy	1002	20%	200
Nuclear safety and safeguards	414	50%	207
Controlled thermonuclear fusion	840	0%	0
Transport	240	10%	24
Targeted socio-economic research (incl. Prospective Technological Institute JRC)			
Cooperation on research with third countries and international organizations	540	20%	108
Dissemination and exploitation of results	330	20%	66
Stimulation of training & mobility of researchers	744	10%	74
TOTAL	12300	30%	3652

(1) An assessment of partnerships between public and private research shows that co-operative networking favours the emergence of innovation. Adapting and widening these intervention arrangements on a national and community scale are decisive means of making the transition towards diversification.

Budget cuts and employmer

Defence budgets for industrialised countries (1)			Internal market (1) equipment	
Country	1984	1992	1984	1992
Germany	25,617	23,771	9,980	8,121
Belgium	2,645	2,206	0,881	0,428
Denmark	2,020	2,016	0,717	0,622
Spain	6,359	5,440	2,412	1,973
France	25,379	26,875	10,752	12,660
Greece	3,264	3,027	1,218	0,858
Ireland	0,414	0,383		
Italy	12,422	15,566	3,727	3,849
Luxembourg				
Netherlands	5,891	5,668	1,607	1,417
Portugal	1,041	1,481	0,209	0,205
United Kingdom	33,722	31,035	15,518	11,782
Total E.C.	118,774	117,467	47,020	41,916
Austria	1,238	1,178	0,276	0,283
Finland	1,847	1,599	0,697	0,734
Norway	2,326	2,677	0,850	0,930
Sweden	4,283	4,148	1,536	1,659
Switzerland	2,940	2,773	1,473	1,375
Total EFTA	12,634	12,376	4,831	4,980
United States (3)	219,186	222,534	109,207	110,035
Canada	7,621	7,746	2,756	2,644
Japan	17,434	23,942	7,187	10,051
General Total	375,648	384,065	171,002	169,626

Source : G Defence. VE1 - (1) expressed in billion constant ECUS 1990 -

ion within the defence sector

Turnover of industry [1]		Export trade [1]		Direct employment in the armament production	
1984	1992	1984	1992 [2]	1984	1992 [2]
11,101	9,034	1,868	1,506	147.000	93.000
1,366	0,527	0,672	0,165	28.000	8.000
0,617	0,587	0,050	0,024	10.000	8.000
3,565	2,499	1,256	0,588	77.000	41.000
16,360	15,467	6,626	3,578	290.000	195.000
0,966	0,472	0,163	0,011	24.000	15.000
5,168	4,224	1,772	0,805	95.000	67.000
1,437	1,432	0,568	0,328	24.000	20.000
0,269	0,190	0,182	0,027	16.000	11.000
19,244	14,390	4,227	3,390	360.000	204.000
60,091	48,822	17,384	10,423	1.071.000	662.000
0,579	0,270	0,350	0,032	12.000	5.000
0,634	0,734	0,054	0,038	10.000	8.000
0,527	0,762	0,044	0,040	10.000	12.000
1,800	2,019	0,425	0,480	24.000	23.000
0,835	1,389	0,261	0,170	12.000	14.000
4,373	5,174	1,135	0,760	68.000	62.000
119,068	123,952	10,313	14,497	1.323.000	1.178.000
3,150	2,894	0,732	0,374	76.000	78.000
6,635	8,968	0,232	0,074	42.000	34.000
193,317	189,809	29,796	26,128	2.580.000	2.014.000

ion - [3] actual expenses (budget outlays)

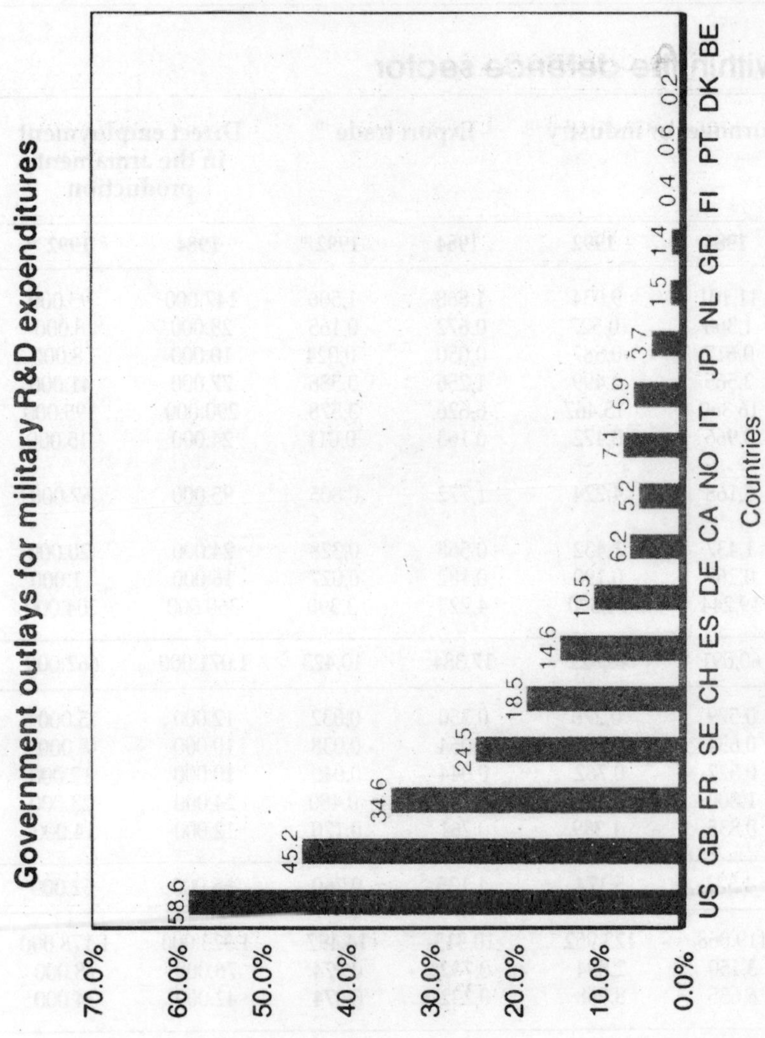
Government outlays for military R&D expenditures
70.0%
60.0%
50.0%
40.0%
30.0%
20.0%
10.0%
0.0%
58.6
45.2
34.6
24.5
18.5
14.6
10.5
6.2
5.2
7.1
5.9
3.7
15
1.4
0.4
0.6
0.2
US GB FR SE CH ES DE CA NO IT JP NL GR FI PT DK BE
Countries
Source: Merit, data: GRIP/STOA

Table 2

Table 3

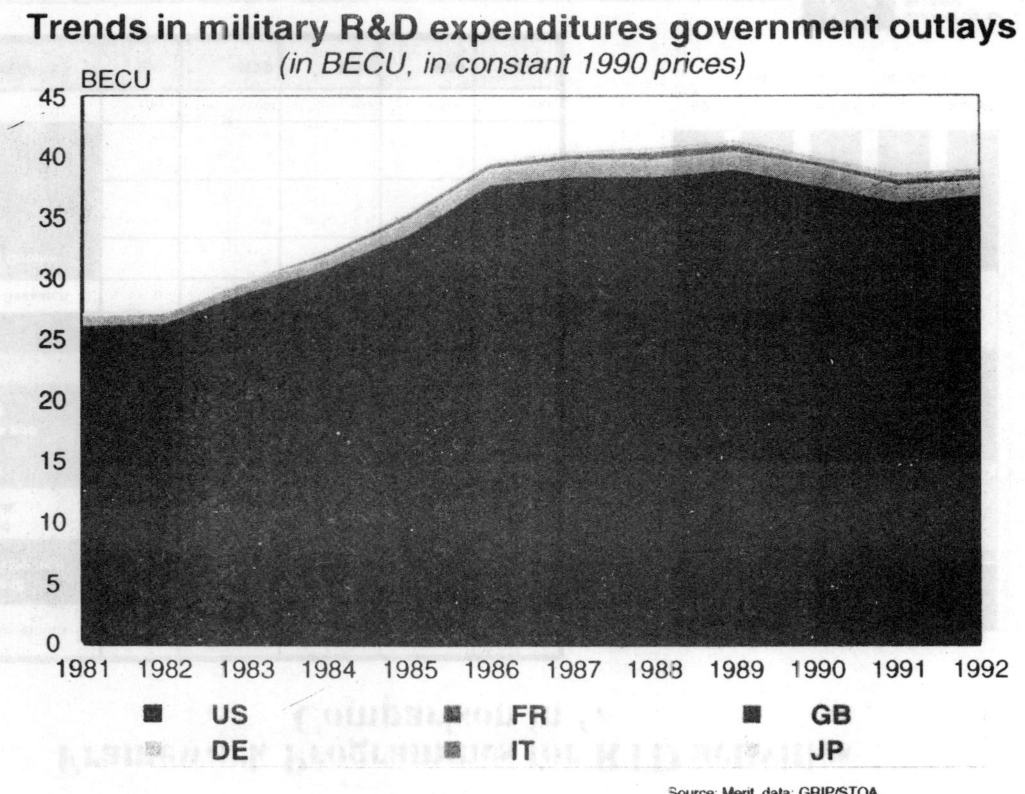
Trends in military R&D expenditures government outlays
(in BECU, in constant 1990 prices)
BECU
45
40
35
30
25
20
15
10
5
0
1981 1982 1983 1984 1985 1986 1987 1988 1989 1990 1991 1992
US
DE
FR
IT
GB
JP
Source: Merit, data: GRIP/STOA

Table 4

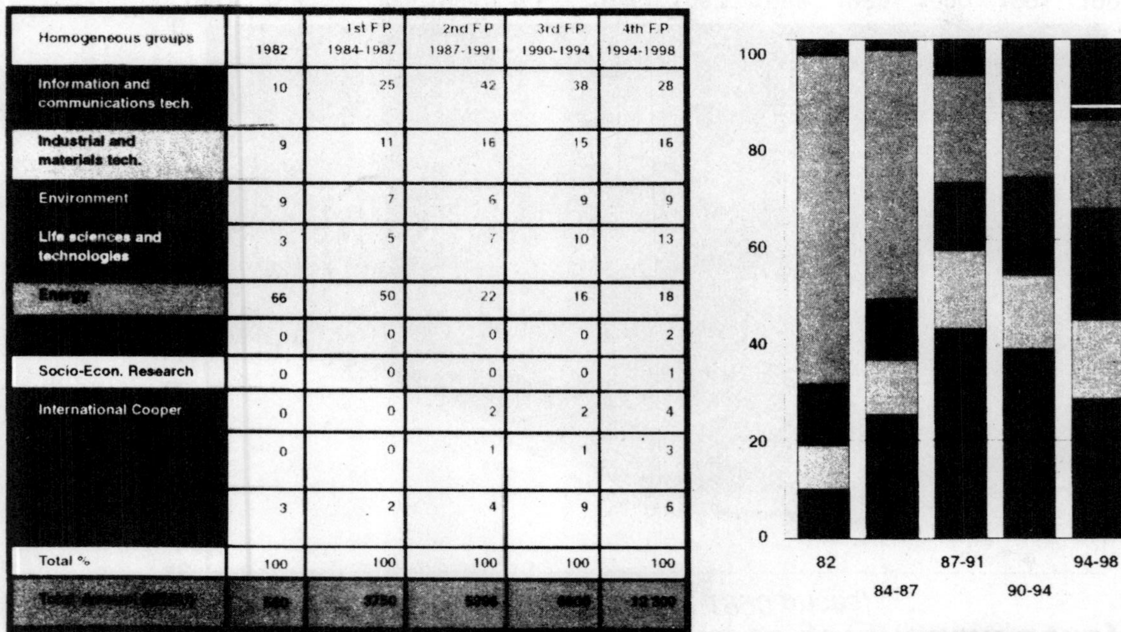

Framework Programmes for RTD activities Comparison in %

Homogeneous groups	1982	1st F.P. 1984-1987	2nd F.P. 1987-1991	3rd F.P. 1990-1994	4th F.P. 1994-1998
Information and communications tech.	10	25	42	38	28
Industrial and materials tech.	9	11	16	15	16
Environment	9	7	6	9	9
Life sciences and technologies	3	5	7	10	13
Energy	66	50	22	16	18
[illegible]	0	0	0	0	2
Socio-Econ. Research	0	0	0	0	1
International Cooper	0	0	2	2	4
[illegible]	0	0	1	1	3
[illegible]	3	2	4	9	6
Total %	100	100	100	100	100
[illegible]	[illegible]	3750	[illegible]	[illegible]	12 300

RTD Policies — European Commission - DG XII Science, Research and Development

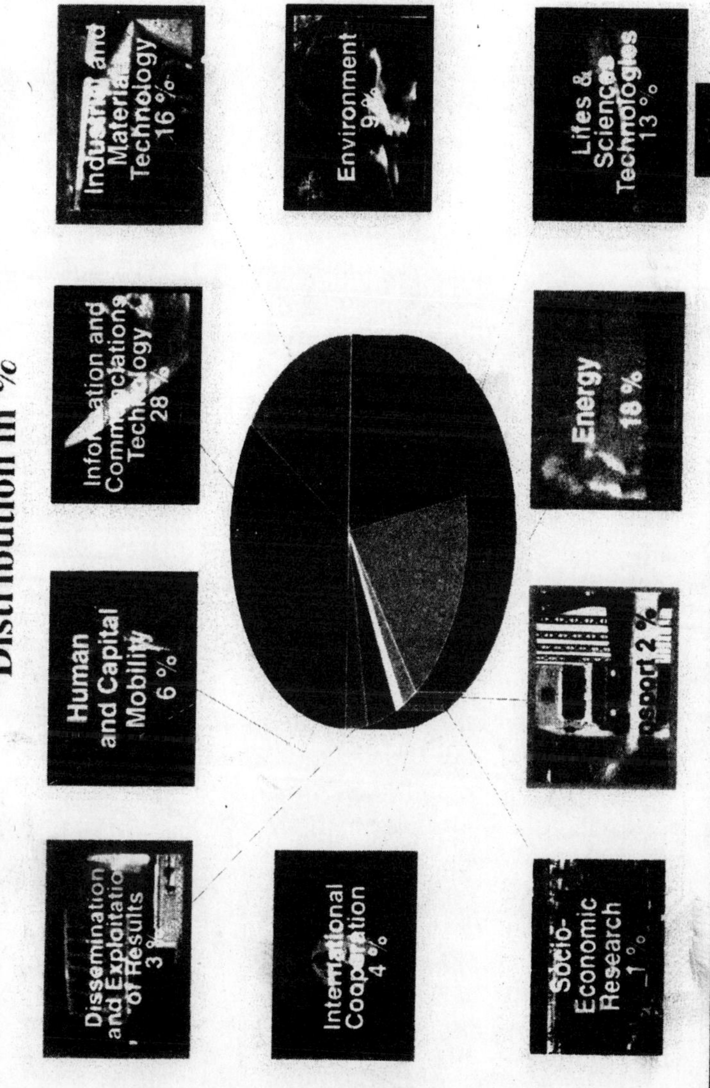
Fourth Framework Programmes (1994-1998)
Distribution in %
Dissemination and Exploitatio of Results 3 %
Human and Capital Mobility 6 %
Information and Communications Technology 28 %
Industrial and Material Technology 16 %
International Cooperation 4 %
Environment 9 %
Socio-Economic Research 1 %
nsport 2 %
Energy 18 %
Lifes & Sciences Technologies 13 %
RTD Policies
European Commission - DG XII Science, Research and Development

Table 5

Table 5

Fourth Framework Programme (1994-1998) Distribution in %

4
An Example of the Utilization of the Military Nuclear Complex for Peaceful Purposes

Pierre Zaleski

1. Introduction

One of the major difficulties in military conversion is to find cases that are realistic from the point of view of:
- politics
- economics
- financing
- society.

In this report, we would like to propose an example which we believe meets the above criteria. The suggestion is to use the manpower, and to some extent the installations (laboratories, factories) of Russia's military nuclear complex to build a small series (8-10) of fast neutron plutonium storage reactor (FNPSR) power stations. These power stations, with a unit output of some 800 megawatts electric, would have two main functions:
- store the excess of Russian military-grade plutonium, and
- produce electricity at competitive prices.

2. Political Aspects

As a result of the agreement on nuclear arms limitation between the US and Russia, there will be available a large quantity of fissile materials. The utilization of highly enriched uranium poses no major problems; the solutions exist and are in the process of implementation.

On the other hand, there is no clear and well-accepted solution for weapons-grade plutonium.

Indeed, there are two opposite attitudes:

- The first is represented by Russia and also by many OECD countries like France, Japan, and the U.K. It can be summarized as follows.

Civilian nuclear energy is an important and very acceptable (from the economic and environmental aspects) source of energy for the long term. It is absolutely necessary to develop nuclear power during the next century if one wishes to satisfy the world needs for energy and especially the developing countries' needs. The other sources of energy — fossil, renewable... — alone, even combined with a substantial effort of energy saving and efficient energy use, will not be sufficient (Refs. 1 and 2).

To achieve this sustained development for the long term, it will be necessary sooner or later, but certainly during the next century, to use more efficiently uranium through the use of plutonium in fast breeder reactors. Therefore, in view of those countries, plutonium is a precious material which sooner or later will be indispensable and, even if for the moment its use for energy production in fast breeder reactors is not economic, it should be preserved for the future. We can observe that plutonium already contributes a very substantial part of the energy produced in light water reactors, where it is formed and burned in situ. It is also used in some countries, notably France, after extraction during reprocessing of standard fuels, and incorporation in mixed-oxide (MOX) fuel and utilized in light water reactors. This last technique is presently only marginally economic.

- The second attitude is represented notably by the U.S. government, and can be summarized as follows.

There is no explicit statement that nuclear energy contribution to world needs will be limited, in fact very limited. But the indirect statements, and most of the actions, of the administraton of President Clinton indicate that nothing is done to ensure the long-term contribution of nuclear energy to world energy needs.

The opposition to the reprocessing of spent nuclear fuel, and endorsement of direct and irretrievable disposal of this fuel, as well as abandonment of all development of fast breeder reactors, clearly indicate that the U.S. administration tends to consider that nuclear energy will play only a very limited role in the future. Indeed, by using present technology light water reactors and without recycling, the world's reasonably assured uranium resources, plus those expected to be recoverable at $130 per kilogram, would produce an energy equivalent of 350 billion barrels of oil. This represents only one-third of the proven resources of oil and gas, and one-thirtieth of the resources of coal (Ref. 3). From this point of view, plutonium is a nuisance, and its only quality—use for nuclear weapons—applied to excess weapons-grade plutonium becomes a major problem and concern. The only preoccupation of the U.S. is how to destroy this plutonium, if possible, and if not, how to safely dispose of it.

The U.S. National Academy of Sciences report on this subject considers two main ways to dispose of this plutonium. One is to incorporate it in MOX fuel and denature it by irradiation in light water reactors, and then dispose of it irretrievably in deep geological storage; the second is to mix it with fission products, and then dispose of the mixture in deep geological, irretrievable storage.

If one considers these two views and tries to apply them to the excess of weapons-grade plutonium in Russia, which may be estimated at some 80-100 tonnes, one has no really good solution:

- contamination by fission products and final disposal is not acceptable for Russia;
- burning it in Russian light water reactors is possible, but far from an optimal solution. It would have the following problems:

a) It would take quite a long time. It would therefore require long temporary storage, which costs money, and is not foolproof from the proliferation viewpoint. For example, with a change of government in Russia, it would be possible to re-use this plutonium at short notice for making weapons.

b) the economics of recycling this plutonium as MOX under Russian conditions must still be demonstrated.

c) It does not completely preserve the plutonium for future uses in breeder reactors, which according to View No. 1, would be the preferable solution for the future.

A third solution has been suggested by the Japanese, namely burning the plutonium in a newly developed fuel (plutonium incorporated in a neutral matrix) in Russian light water reactors. This technique has not been demonstrated, and its economics are far from clear; it is also contrary to the idea that the plutonium shall be preserved for future uses.

Our proposal consists in building FNPSR reactors with an internal breeding ratio close to 1, no blanket, and with rather low specific power — some 10 to 15 kg of Pu per MWe — using large-diameter fuel rods.

These reactors, fueled with weapons-grade plutonium, shall be designed to obtain a very long residence time for fuel, up to 10-20 years. This solution may satisfy the U.S. point of view, because plutonium in an operating fast reactor core is safe and more difficult for re-use in warheads than is plutonium stored in retrievable safeguarded storage.

It may also satisfy Russia, since with a breeding ratio near 1, after full burnup, the quantity of plutonium recovered and available for future use will be substantially similar to the original quantity. It may also satisfy countries like France, Japan, and the U.K., since this solution gives on the one hand the safest storage for Russian weapons-grade plutonium while producing electricity at a competitive price (see following paragraph) and maintaining knowhow and increasing operating experience with fast neutron power stations, useful for future FBR development.

After the maximum burnup is achieved (10-20 years), the following options would be possible:

- exchange Russian plutonium "denatured" in spent fuel for U.S. weapons-grade plutonium, and use the latter for the second load of the FNPSR stations.
- reprocess the spent fuel and re-use the plutonium in the same reactors.
- store the denatured plutonium in safeguarded, retrievable storage for future use, and use civilian plutonium for the second fuel load.

After two or three fuel cycles are done in the FNPSR and the reactors have reached the end of their useful life, one will have to choose one of the following solutions:

1. If the American view prevails, definitively dispose of Pu in underground storage, or if American views still prevail but environmental concerns dictate it, burn the Pu in fast burner reactors (See Ref. 4, Capra program).

2. If the first attitude prevails and nuclear energy is developed, use this Pu in fast neutron breeder reactors.

3. If the conditions are still not clear 40-50 years from now, store the plutonium in a new series of FNPSR power stations. This would preserve all options open and the decision would be made in a clearer context.

One of the important aspects of this kind of project is timing. For our idea, we could imagine the following schedule: 10 years for development and validation of the concept, notably fuel irradiation; however, the start of construction of the first reactors could be envisaged before all experimental results are in hand, for example, seven years after the start of the project.

Duration of construction could be estimated at 5-6 years, and one could conceive construction starts every year on three reactor units. With these rather optimistic assumptions, the total project would take some 15 years. Considering that this dismantlement of plutonium warheads will likely come after dismantlement of uranium 235 warheads and that one will need the plutonium for fabrication of first fuel loads for FNPSR some 8 years after the beginning of the project, the above schedule is rather consistent with safe disposal of military plutonium.

3. Technical Aspects

With plutonium value of zero or negative—indeed, the owner of plutonium may pay some fee for storage which otherwise is not free (safeguards)—one has to reoptimize fast neutron breeder cores. The natural idea is to tend in the fast neutron plutonium storage cores to use as much plutonium per MWe as possible, in view to store more Pu per MWe and also to increase the diameter of fuel rods, decreasing the relative contribution of fuel fabrication to thc total cost of a kilowatt-hour. It is also natural to increase the residence time of fuel in-reactor, in view to simplify fuel handling equipment without penalizing the availability factor.

In achieving these objectives, one will get a higher Doppler coefficient, which plays a positive role in controlling power excursions, but one will also get a more positive sodium void coefficient, which has an adverse effect on safety. One will also get a higher internal breeding ratio necessary to allow longer residence time by minimizing the reactivity changes.

One will, therefore, have to optimize the core to ensure an overall safe behavior. To do this, one can for example design a relatively flat core and ensure proper design of the upper plenum so that any sodium voiding of a section of core will inevitably lead to sodium voiding of the corresponding section of the upper plenum, where the reactivity effect can be designed to be negative.

In addition, it seems reasonable to limit the size of the core by limiting the total output of each power unit. A reasonable value would be between 600 and 800 MWe. We may note that these values correspond to well-developed technology in Russia. The BN-600 fast breeder reactor has been operating very successfully for over 10 years, with an availability that is among the best in Russia, but also among the best in the world, all types of nuclear plants considered. Its average availability over 10 years was 97.5%, with a capacity factor of 71%.

In addition, Russia has developed detailed projects for the BN-800 fast breeder reactor type, directly inspired from BN-600 technology (Ref. 5). Therefore, with some cooperation from western Europe (Phenix, Superphenix, EFR projects) and Japan (Monju), Russian scientists and technicians should be able to design and build without too much development a safe 800-MW fast neutron power station.

The optimization of core mentioned above, the development and fabrication of Pu-bearing fuel with large diameter rods, will require close collaboration with western countries, notably with France, which has more experience in Pu-bearing fuel than Russia.

This last domain — core and fuel — is the most innovative for the FNPSR design, and will probably require the most R&D.

The typical goals for the design may be:

- fuel rod diameter about twice that used in present breeder

designs;
- specific power in the range of 10-15 kg Pu per MWe;
- internal breeding ratio in the range of 0.9 to 1.0;
- residence time of fuel in the reactor, 10-20 years.

4. Economics Aspects

Even if the project shall for pragmatic reasons be closely related to the Russian BN-800 project, we will base our discussion of economic aspects first on the very recent (1993) EFR study carried out by utilities and manufacturers from France, Germany and the U.K., since as far as we know this is the most recent, serious and pertinent study.

This study (Ref. 6) shows that in a western European context, a series of 1,500-MW FBRs, taking a plutonium value of zero, can be in the range of economic competitivity with LWRs, as least with some uncertainty margin.

This series of FBRs was not optimized for plutonium storage; therefore, one can hope that some gains could be obtained due to:

1. simplified fuel handling equipment design (fuel handling every 10 to 20 years);
2. much lower cost of fuel cycle. The large fuel rod diameter makes it possible to produce more energy per rod (for example 4 times as much), and the cost of fuel rod fabrication should not be very sensitive to the diameter;
3. potential fees to be paid by plutonium owners (for the storage function).

Thus these gains should lead in the EFR context to a situation very competitive with LWRs.

This result should be transposable to the Russian context, provided a well-planned construction of a series of identical plants is considered (8-10 800-MW units).

There may, however, be one penalizing point, namely, the 800-MW size, which was originally selected for core design and local pragmatic reasons (the existence of BN-600 and of a detailed project for BN-800).

This size is much smaller than the 1,450-MW contemplated in the EFR studies, and slightly smaller than the typical modern Russian LWR of 1,000 MW. The economic penalty for size effect should probably not exceed the advantage due to the re-optimization of the EFR core (see above).

One can therefore expect that this project has a good potential for competitivity with LWR projects in Russia, that is, that it could produce electricity at the same price.

5. *Financial Aspects*

The need for new electric power plants in Russia is quite evident. Even if the domestic demand is not growing, because of the development of energy saving and efficient energy use, the possibility of exports to neighboring countries and the need to replace older power plants, nuclear or not, justifies new construction.

However, because of the difficult economic situation in Russia, international financing seems necessary, at least for the major part of a plant, and at the same time appears to be possible. Indeed, the international community, and especially OECD countries, should be interested in resolving the problems of the safe storage of weapons-grade plutonium, and some of the OECD countries should be interested in maintaining world expertise and increasing operational experience in fast neutron reactor power plants, and the entire international community in helping the Russian economy in its effort of reconstruction.

A potential additional motivation may exist if Russian authorities accept to link the building of these new plants with decommissioning of older and less-safe nuclear power plants.

All this being said, the important question is how Russia can reimburse the money borrowed for these projects.

What will certainly reassure potential lenders is a contract expressing the reimbursement in a commodity exported normally by Russia, which has well-established international value and which is in demand in the lending countries, for example, natural gas.

The other advantage to link the reimbursement to gas is that Russia can consider that it saves gas when producing electricity with new plant, and reimburses only part of the saved gas.

Let us make some very simplified back-of-envelope calculations, which have no other intention than to indicate some trends.

In a French Ministry of Industry study (Ref. 7), the costs of a kilowatt-hour produced on the one hand by a combined-cycle natural gas plant and on the other hand by a nuclear plant are analyzed. The plants are assumed to be in operation in the year 2003, and the discount rate is 8% for zero inflation. The capital cost (amortization and interest charges) of a 1,400-MW LWR plant expressed per Kwh produced by the plant operated in baseload mode represents some 64% of the cost of natural gas in France necessary to produce one Kwh in a combined-cycle gas plant operating in the baseload mode, assuming a low (conservative) hypothesis for gas prices at the beginning of the next century.

If one assumes that a FNPSR power plant of 800 MW will have an overall capital cost of 1.3 times that of a 1,400-MW LWR plant in France (the 30% extra cost being compensated by cheaper fuel cycle cost), the amortization and interest charge for this plant will represent 83% of the cost of natural gas needed to generate the same number of Kwh.

In fact, as some eminent Russian scientists (Ref. 8) have indicated, in the present situation and for a given amount of dollars or other hard currency, the Russian nuclear industry may perform much more work than western industry. For some specific examples related to the upgrading of old Russian reactors, they indicate a factor of 16 for the cost-efficiency of Russian versus western industry.

Even if we may consider this factor as applicable only to some specific situations, it would not be extraordinary to consider a factor of two to four - let us say three - to characterize the relative cost-efficiencies of the two industries (Russian and western). This may be due to the relative low cost of labor in Russia expressed in hard currency, as well as the high contribution of labor costs in the total cost of nuclear construction.

If we assume that at least 75% of work for construction of FNPSR stations could and would be done by Russian industry, we would then have a cost expressed in hard currency and in percentage of typical western costs for the same work equal to: 75%/3 + 25% = 50%.

In this context, it would suffice to devote 41.5% of the gas saved to the payment of interest at 8% and amortization of the capital cost.

We have taken 8% for the interest rate from the French study (Ref. 7). This is a rather high rate, but can be rationalized by considering that it includes some risk factor for political and economic uncertainties in Russia.

This back-of-envelope calculation indicates that construction of such reactors with western financing secured by Russian gas sales may be quite advantageous financially for Russia as well as acceptable for western lenders, such as some OECD countries and/or the EBRD and the European Union.

The total amount of financing — which should be less than $10 billion if our hypotheses are correct, notably about the cost of construction in Russia — should not be out of line with the possibilities of the potential lenders.

6. Societal Aspects

Any major conversion of industry poses social problems, especially when it includes large training programs and / or major relocation of workforce.

In the case we have proposed, there is no necessity of major retraining - perhaps some connected with transformation of plutonium warheads into plutonium-bearing fuel elements, but this task has only limited impact on the total project.

Relocation of workforce should be quite minor. The idea is to use existing laboratories, development institutes, and factories, necessitating little or no relocation of staff.

The actual construction of power plants would not impose site constraints different from those for other kinds of nuclear plants; it could take place on the sites already considered in Russian government plans for FBR plants. Therefore, it would not introduce specific problems of relocation of construction personnel as compared with regular practices of the industry.

There remains the problem of public opinion, which should be treated with appropriate attention. However, provided the safety standards are impeccable and proper information efforts are deployed to explain the advantages of a non-polluting electric power plant, and provided that the local population receives tangible benefits from this development, this problem should be solvable.

Indeed, a project transforming weapons material into useful energy should have some attraction for people.

In conclusion, we believe that this idea deserves a thorough study.

REFERENCES

1. STARR, CHAUNCEY, MILTON F. SEARL, and S.Y. ALPERT, 1992, "Energy Sources: A Realistic Outlook." Science 256, 981-987
2. *Energy for Tomorrow's World.* World Energy Council, 34 St. James' Street, London SW1A 1HD, U.K., December 1993.
3. DAVIS, W. KENNETH, "The Future of Nuclear Power: The Fast Breeder Reactor." Paper presented at the Dixie Lee Ray Memorial Symposium on Science-Based Environmental Management, Seattle, Wash., August 31, 1994.
4. "Le Projet Capra: Enjeux et Objectifs." Note de présentation du Commissariat à l'Energie Atomique, 29-33, rue de la Fédération, 75015 Paris, France. 6 June 1994.
5. SLESAREV. I. "Stratégie des Réacteurs Rapides: Russie." in *Les Centrales à Neutrons Rapides: Quel Avenir?* Centre de Géopolitique de l'Energie et des Matières Premières, Université de Paris Dauphine, Place de Lattre de Tassigny, 75776 Paris France. 1994.
6. *EFR - European Fast Reactor.* EFR Associates, 10 rue Juliette Récamier, B.P. 3087 F, 69398 Lyon Cedex 03, France.
7. *Les Coûts de Référence - Production d'Electricite d'Origine Thermique.* Ministère de l'Industrie, des Postes et des Télécommunications, et du Commerce Extérieur, DGEMP-DIGEC, Service de l'Electricité, Paris, 1993
8. PONOMAREV-STEPNOY, N. and E. ADAMOV, in *Proceedings of the MIEC-CGEMP seminar: La sécurité de l'approvisionnement en énergie de l'Europe - Rôle de la Russie.* Paris, France, March 1994. Centre de Géopolitique de l'Energie et des Matières Premières, Université Paris-Dauphine (see Ref. 5).

PARTICULAR CASES OF MILITARY CONVERSION AND ITS IMPACTS ON SCIENCE AND TECHNOLOGY

5
Military Conversion and Science from a Global Perspective

John Proctor

We are still in the midst of momentous changes begun in the late 1980s which are continuing principally in Europe and the former Soviet Union, as well as in the rest of the world. These changes will have great impact upon political, economic and social conditions of most of the people of earth. For many of us, the impact upon the present state and future development of science is the issue.

Background

In Russian and Eastern European science, most of the state support of sciences has disappeared. Newspapers tell us it is because of a great economic crisis. But my visits there strengthen my belief that profound reconsiderations are underway of the place science is to have in the former Soviet states and countries of Eastern Europe. Civilian and military leaders of massive military oriented programs were lavish in their support of basic hard science, key technologies and supporting disciplines. After the political and economic collapse of the Soviet state, hard science lost support; "Big Science" projects stopped, and as for the soft sciences, they appear to be struggling and gasping for credibility and support. [1. UNESCO-ROSTE Seminar, 1990.]

In the United States as in Europe and the former Soviet Union, the "Peace Dividend" has not materialized for science and technology funding. Basic science is financially supported by nation states and that support has been weakened in the face of competing demands upon political decision makers.

The Russian Federation's funding of the Russian Academy of Sciences with its over 300,000 employees, dozens of institutes, libraries, test sites, observatories, publishing houses, research ships and planes has been cut from 3 to 5 times in comparable terms according to Kaptiza. [2. S. P. Kapitza, 1994.] Coupled with inflation of over 4000% in the last two years, the compensation of scientists, technicians, architects and medical doctors is ridiculously low. Youngsters are not entering science and technical careers; scientists are leaving science. Some say. "Fine. Science in the USSR was top heavy and overstuffed. Let the dismantling continue." Others say the pillaging of the former USSR and Eastern Block science is ridiculous, sadistic, or downright stupid in the face of possible nuclear proliferation, not to mention chemical and biological threats. Ignoring the promises of their science in bio-technology, advances in rocketry, mathematics, optics, and lasers is simply irrational.

The United States Department of Defense budget for Research and Development in 1991 was $30 billion in 1995 dollars. In 1995, it is $26 billion and by 1999, it is budgeted at $21 billion in 1995 dollars, a minus 30% change from 1991! [3. U.S. Congress, Congressional Budget Office, 1994.] The private sector will have to increase its financial support of science and technology and that in turn, depends upon controlled economic growth. Having to depend upon open market forces to provide financial support for science and technology is risky indeed.

Military Conversion

The problems of defense conversion and brain drain provides a uniting global issue for learned societies, academies of art and science, and organizations advancing technology around the world to maintain pressure on decision makers to raise science and technology in their scheme of priorities.

While government at any level generally seeks to control and constrain organizations, science, engineering, and technology organizations strive to open, share, and recognize the contributions of genius, innovation and hard work. For example, the Washington Academy of Sciences is focusing on its role as science advocate, communicator, and supporter of our Junior Academy of Science. We are clearly awed by the magnitude of scientist migration and the realization that while this is occurring in our increasingly complex world, the numbers of scientists and technologists coping with problems of humankind appear not to be increasing. A new form of apartheid may be developing in terms of the capacity to do brain work - a form of imposed segregation undermining humankind's security, health and quality of life.

Defense or military conversion, in my view, is a subset of the larger brain drain problems. It is not a scientific question per se but rather a matter for scientists to explore. Thus, the first question, always the most important, is what paradigm or concept formulation promises the most utility?

The problem of defense conversion and, to a certain extent brain drain, it seems to me, is a matter of business. That is taking joint venture risks in bringing technologies to market while governments continue support of basic science and education.

The paradigm I have been suggesting for the past three years is one that emphasizes incentives to encourage the reallocation of resources and would be essentially a cooperative effort between government and private business. The use of incentives in a defense conversion paradigm encourages the retention of critical military skills and facilitates the separation of those who need to be converted through training or direct absorption into the civilian occupation pool. Obvious incentives are pay, allowances, interesting work, relocation assistance, housing and living subsidies and educational opportunities.

Similarly, incentives are needed to maintain civilian skills, encourage individuals in surplus jobs to seek training and to help workers shift to jobs with other employers. Finally, incentives [4. G. W. Miller, 1992] are needed for employers to stabilize the civilian occupation pool in critical areas such as science, technology and medical practice.

Priorities based upon a census by scientific and technical occupation in the states of the former Soviet Union and the Eastern European countries would provide an important ingredient for conversion strategies which would involve sustainable contracts, the fostering of innovation, and focus on technical institutes, inter alia. [5. National Science Board, 1991.] Now here is a particularly difficult problem...setting priorities. As Judge Brazelon of the U.S. District Court has said: "The equal treatment of unequals is the greatest inequality of all". Whose fairness?.....What objectives? These issues are discussed in my paper in a recent issue of the Journal of the Washington Academy of Sciences. [6. J. H. Proctor, 1992.]

The implementation in Russia of defense conversion strategies within a paradigm of incentives would require some new functions at the national, regional and local levels, such as "broker centers" for job posting, job application referral and hiring, employment agreements and negotiation assistance. Investment allocation decisions in terms of how much, to whom, for how long, would require decision support processes to be installed in Russia and Eastern Europe where there is no history of such investment/incentives; a most difficult aspect of any implementation. Program evaluation and feedback to decision makers on the paradigm's implementation is the final step before repeating steps in different ways, at different speeds, in different socio-economic and geographical locations. I am pleased to observe that the partnership of the Russian Federation's Ministry of Science and Technology and the Russian Academy of Sciences is rapidly evolving.

Case 1: U.S. Aerospace

In the United States, the U.S. aerospace industry provides an example of an industry coping with defense cuts, a weak global economy and increased international competition. The U.S. aerospace industry is a critical part of our country's domestic and export economies. It accounts for more than 25 percent of all of the nation's research and development expenditures and is the country's leader in R&D spending on new technologies [7. Aerospace Industries Association of America, 1994]. Industry shipments are forecast to drop 11% in real terms to $92.3 billion in 1994 and exports to decline 15% to $34 billion. Employment in Aerospace companies will continue to be cut back as military programs end, are reduced or delayed.

As part of the new spirit of cooperation between the Russian and American aerospace industries, an agreement was reached in September of 1993 to construct a space station blending elements of the U.S. Freedom and Russian Mir projects. Another product of Russian aerospace collaboration is the four engine, long range aircraft, IL-96M. It will be powered by U.S. built Pratt and Whitney engines and fitted with U.S. advanced avionics. The Tupolev's TU-204, mid-range, 200 seat twin jet airliner will be powered by Rolls-Royce engines.

Case 2: Brain Drain in Russia

Military conversion in Russia could be a forcing function to accelerate or increase "intellectual emigration or Brain Drain."

The exodus on a massive scale of researchers, teachers and lecturers, engineers and technicians is producing actual damage to the national economies of the CIS and Eastern European countries. Estimates show that at the beginning of 1991 losses due to emigration of scientists and engineers from the CIS amounted to nearly 100bn rubles. If we add the calculations of UN experts that the emigration of one specialist of this category produces damage of about US $300,000 to his/her country. In terms of dollars, this means that emigration of scholars and engineers might bring an annual potential loss of US $60-75bn to the CIS countries. [8. S. J. Simanovsky, 1993]. From 1992 to the year 2000 the loss would be in excess of half a trillion dollars.

Steps to limit intellectual migration and promote successful defense conversion and the re-engineering of military industries depend upon job creation and innovative talent utilization programs. Such steps as international conferences; three month to three year temporary visits or sabbaticals; cooperative forms of basic research; joint ventures in technology application; scientific and teacher exchanges, and computer linkages are all positive. UNESCO has set up a "fund for basic science in Russia". Model cooperative agreements have been reached between the Russian Academy of Sciences and western organization such as AT&T, Corning, and the Soros Foundation. These steps to encourage positive mobility help avoid returning to a totalitarian state and the violation of basic human rights and freedoms as articulated by the United Nations. [9. Ministry of Science and Technology of the Russian Federation, 1994.] I personally am greatly encouraged by the current leadership of the Russian Academy of Sciences who support international cross fertilization of teams and institutions thereby reducing the likelihood of the re-emergence of the old fiefdoms and closed organizational structures that existed without accountability.

Personal Observations

What really breaks my heart when key members of the academic community leave, is when books on science, technology, architecture, law, medicine and theology cease to be published;

when the continuity of research and teaching is lost and young minds lose mentors. [10. Scientific American, 1993.] We should also grieve for the unborn ideas and unrealized experimental plans.

I feel obliged also to stress the importance of moral factors in times of difficulty. In the face of adversity, the loss of courage and morale is a most significant feature. Anti-intellectual trends are now openly expressed in the United States. In Russian and Eastern European media, now freed of censorship and with a newly found responsibility of the press to society, "money makers" are the new heroes. Coupled with strident expressions of nationalism, anti-semitism, and anti-religion, it all combines to place fuel on the fires of frustration and despair, especially among the young. Fewer of the best and brightest enter math and science classes and careers, even more leave their jobs in research labs and university classrooms for business. The Russians call this "internal brain drain"and it must be added to intellectual migration to estimate losses. Boris Vinogradov, Russian Federation Commission for UNESCO estimates that 27% of scientific personnel in Russia (in some regions 50%) transferred to commercial ventures in 1992. [11. B. Vinogradov, 1993.]

Conclusion

Learned societies and academies both non-governmental and government supported have clear roles in defense conversion and related issues of brain drain. [12. National Academy of Sciences, 1992.] These roles, as seen by the Washington Academy of Sciences and the World Academy of Art and Science, consist of (i) increasing public awareness of global issues facing science, (ii) encouraging young people to enter and stay in their chosen courses of higher education, and (iii) developing strategies with our fellows in foreign Academies of Science and Technology. These three roles are compatible with or perhaps, in addition to, its Members and Fellows providing advice and council to decision makers. I cannot overemphasize the need for us individually and collectively to combat anti-technological, anti-scientific, anti-intellectual trends which have been seen and heard in many places in North America, Europe and Asia. I would also encourage all of us to speak out on these issues and breathe life into them with passion and indignation.

One exemplary effort many of you know about is the televised forum from Washington, DC on April 4, 1993 sponsored by the World Academy of Art and Science, the Russian Academy of Science, and the Washington Academy of Sciences. Fellows of the World Academy of Art and Science from Russia and the US discussed global issues facing humankind to the year 2050. Of particular interest in this project was the willingness of imminent scientists to hold discussions before a large, live audience which included over 125 young students of the Metropolitan Area Washington Junior Academy of Science. We have now made video tapes in Russian and English of this discussion and prepared a book of selected papers by participants. These materials are available to our Fellows for use with young students. The Russian Academy of Sciences is using the video tape and books with middle school students in Russia. We're proud of this program and ask you to help it continue.

Our challenge is clear: to design and implement structures and processes for the modern world to deal with high technology, basic and applied science with the attendant great concentration of power and resources. People look to us to recommend revised procedures for funding transitional structures and processes for science. Nation states which prosper in the long run are those which earlier invested in research, particularly fundamental research. These procedures are needed now. I am personally concerned with the ethics and values of multi-national corporations and international art and science organizations in these matters. Again, whose values? Where will these values come from? Who is holding whom accountable? I urge all who would be helpers to facilitate positive defense conversion to proceed with caution and with respect to avoid worsening the very situation that the West is trying to improve.

REFERENCES

1. UNESCO-ROSTE (Regional Office for Science and Technology for Europe, 1261/A Dorsoduro, Venice, Italy 30123) 1990. Report of the Working Party on Brain Drain Issues in Europe, Lisbon, Portugal, 26-28 November 1990. I. O. Angell and V. A. Kouzminov (eds.), technical report no.3.
2. KAPITZA, S. P., The Future of Russian Science and Science in Eastern Europe, a paper under preparation, Spring, 1994.
3. U. S. Congress, Congressional Budget Office, "Restructuring And Consolidating Defense Support Activities", Table 2. Department of Defense Funding by Major Program, Page 8, July, 1994.
4. MILLER, G.W. 1992, Interim report, Redeploying Assets of the Russian Defense Sector to the Civilian Economy. (Chair. National Academy of Sciences Committee on Enterprise Management in a Market Economy under Defense Conversion.) Washington, D.C. 20219, USA.
5. National Science Board. 1991. Science and Engineering Indicators. 10th edn. US Government Printing Office, Washington, DC 20219, USA.
6. PROCTOR, JOHN H. A Theoretical Basis for Intentional Organizational Change with Comments from a Thirty Year Perspective, Journal of the Washington Academy of Sciences, Volume 82, Number 1, Pages 1-18, March 1992.
7. Aerospace Industries Association of America, Inc., U. S. Industrial Outlook, "Aerospace Facts and Figures, 1993-1994", Chapter 20, Pages 20-1 to 20-5.
8. SIMANOVSKY, STANISLAV. Brain Drain from the Former Soviet Union and the Position of the International Community, Commission of the Russian Federation for UNESCO, Moscow, the Russian Federation presented at the UNESCO-ROSTE Seminar, 25-27 April 1993, Venice, Italy, pages 407-418.
9. Ministry of Science and Technical Policy of the Russian Federation, Committee on "Brain Drain" Problem Under the Commission of the Russian Federation For UNESCO 1994, "Brain Drain" From Russia: Problems, Perspectives and Ways of Regulation, A Seminar and Report, Moscow, 21-23 February, 1994.
10. Scientific American, 1993. Trends in Russian Science. February.
11. VINOGRADOV, BORIS, "Brain Drain in Russia in 1991-92", presented at the UNESCO-ROSTE Seminar, 25-27, April 1993, Venice, Italy, pages 203-210.
12. National Academy of Sciences, 1992. "Reorientation of the Research Capability of the Former Soviet Union." A Report of the Assistant for Science and Technology to the President of the United States. 13 March.

6
The Finmeccanica Experience in Military Conversion

Angelo Airaghi and Carlo Corsi

FINMECCANICA

ANSALDO   Elsag Bailey

Aerospace, Defense, Energy, Transportation, Automation

FINMECCANICA: THE GROUP

OPERATING STRUCTURE

AERONAUTICS	RADARS AND SYSTEMS	MISSILES	DEFENSE	HELICOPTERS	SERVICE AUTOMATION
SPACE	ELECTRONIC EQUIPMENTS	ENERGY	TRANSPORT	INDUSTRIAL AUTOMATION	OTHERS

FINMECCANICA: THE GROUP

THE DEFENCE ACTIVITIES INVOLVE SEVEN AREAS

VEHICLES	RADAR AND SYSTEMS	MISSILES	WEAPON SYSTEMS	HELICOPTERS	SERVICE AUTOMATION
SPACE AND TELECOMMUNIC	ELECTRONICS EQUIPMENT	ENERGY	TRANSPORTATION	INDUSTRIAL AUTOMATION	OTHERS

PARTLY DEFENCE

FULLY DEFENCE

FULLY COMMERCIAL

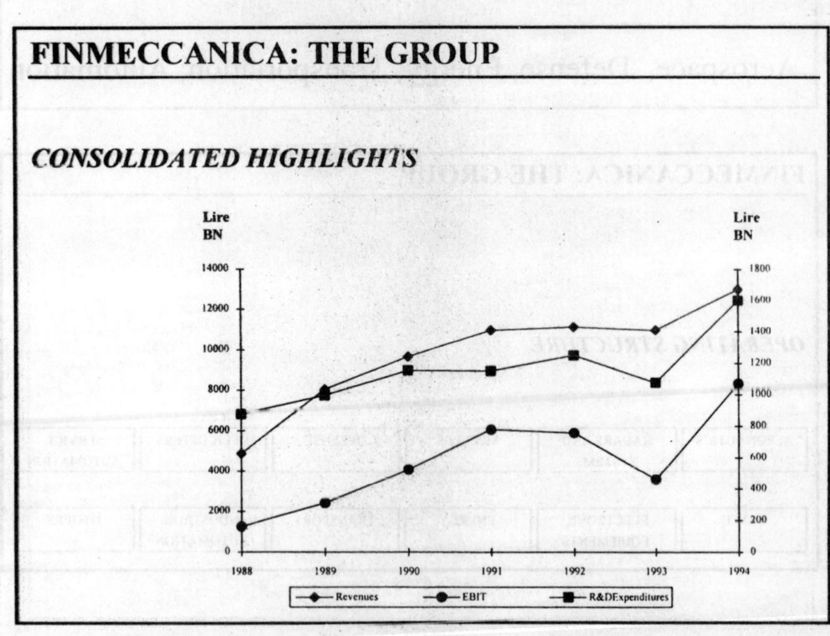

FINMECCANICA: THE GROUP

THE DEFENCE ACTIVITIES REPRESENT 30% OF THE TOTAL TURNOVER

REVENUES BY BUSINESS AREA (1994)

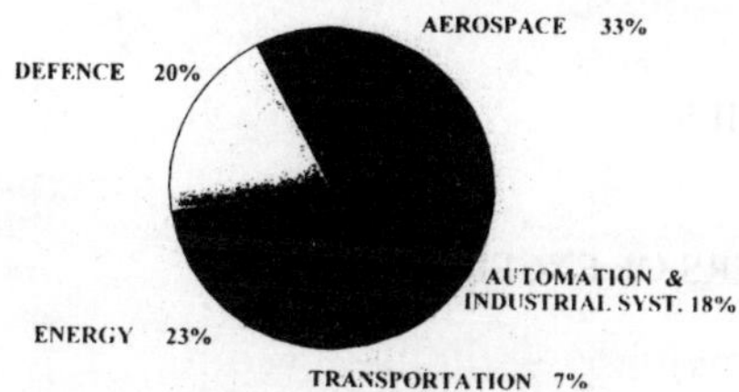

FINMECCANICA: THE GROUP

INTERNATIONALIZATION IS GROWING

FINMECCANICA REVENUES (1994)

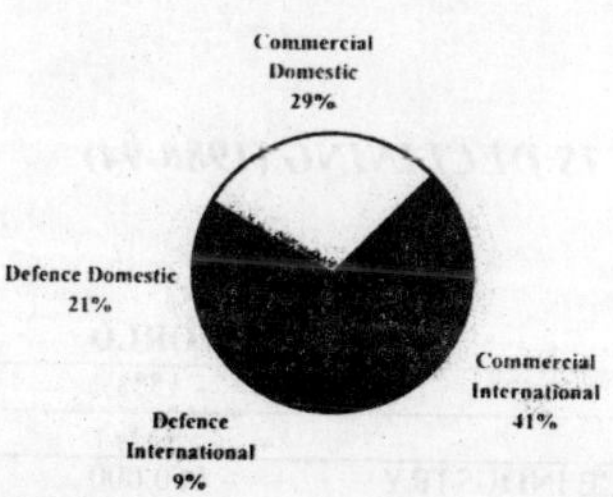

PUSHED BY THE COMMERCIAL ACTIVITIES

FINMEÇCANICA: THE GROUP

R&D - COSTS, STAFF & LABS (1993)

- 7000 FULLY DEDICATED PEOPLE
- 100 LABORATORIES
- SEVERAL CENTERS OF EXCELLENCE
- COSTS: 1 BN $ (1994) OF WHICH::
  - 25% PRELIMINARY AND FINALIZED ACTIVITIES
  - 75% DEVELOPMENT ACTIVITIES

THE DEFENCE MARKET

THE DEFENCE MARKET IS DECLINING (1988-94)

	WORLD	ITALY
DEFENCE BUDGETS	- 15%	- 9%
INVESTMENTS	- 45%	- 55%
EMPLOYMENT IN THE DEFENCE INDUSTRY	- 660.000	- 20.000

THE DEFENCE MARKET: IMPLICATIONS FOR INDUSTRY

1. SMALLER PRODUCTION VOLUMES

2. DECLINE IN R&D PUBLIC EXPENDITURES

3. LESS PROGRAMS

THE DEFENCE MARKET: THE INDUSTRY'S CHALLENGE

HOW TO SURVIVE AND KEEP ALIVE THE HIGH TECH CONTENT

CONVERSION IS, IN PRINCIPLE, NOT VIABLE

DIVERSIFICATION DOES NOT, AGAIN IN PRINCIPLE, DEFEND THE HIGH TECH CONTENT

THE DEFENCE MARKET: THE INDUSTRY REPLY

1. **VS SMALLER VOLUMES ....**

CONCENTRATION, THROUGH M&A

a) THE NATIONAL CHAMPIONS

b) THE INTERNATIONAL AGREEMENTS

THE DEFENCE MARKET: THE INDUSTRY REPLY

2. **VS LESS R&D EXPENDITURES ....**

DEVELOPMENT OF A "COMMON" TECHNOLOGICAL BASE:

a) PUSH THE DUAL USE

b) COMMERCIAL UTILIZATION OF DEFENCE TECHNOLOGIES

THE DEFENCE MARKET: THE INDUSTRY REPLY

3. VS LESS PROGRAMS ....

RESTRUCTURING OF THE R&D DEPTS
(INTEGRATION DEF. AND COMM. ACTIVITIES)

CONVERGENCE BETWEEN COMMERCIAL AND MILITARY REQUIREMENTS

THE DEFENCE MARKET: THE CHALLENGE

SIMPLE STRATEGIES BUT DIFFICULT IMPLEMENTATIONS

LESSONS FROM THE PRACTICAL EXPERIENCE

FINMECCANICA: EXAMPLES

DUAL USE

- HELICOPTERS:
  EH 101: AGUSTA / WESTLAND
  A 129: AGUSTA
- AIRPLANES
  ATR 52 C ALENIA / AEROSPATIALE

FINMECCANICA: EXAMPLES

CONVERGENCE OF REQUIREMENTS

- AIR TRAFFIC CONTROL AND RADARS
- GPS

FINMECCANICA PRACT EXP

STRUCTURES RESHAPING

- ALENIA AERONAUTICS DIVISION
- ALENIA RADARS & SYSTEMS DIVISION

FINMECCANICA: EXAMPLES

TECHNOLOGIES MIGRATION

- ELECTROMAGNETIC COMPATIBILITY
- IMAGING
- HIGH PERFORMANCE COMPUTING
- CRYPTOGRAPHY
- ....
- ....

SOME CRITICAL ASPECT AND CONTRADICTIONS

7
Military Conversion and its Impacts on Science and Technology: Elements of the Italian Case

Fulvia Farinelli and Giulio Perani

1. Introduction: the Italian System of Innovation

Italy represents one of the success stories of post-war economic growth. Over the past forty years, GNP growth has been higher in Italy than in most other industrialized countries. Similarly, productivity and income per capita have risen rapidly and manufacturing exports have increased considerably. In a relatively short period of time Italy has transformed from an agricultural and semindustrialized country to an advanced industrial economy. In addition, during the 1980's it experienced high growth rates in R&D (see table 1), although Italian international specialization remains mainly in traditional products such as textile and shoes, as well as in mechanics and industrial equipment.

Why in Italy did the R&D growth of the 1980s not translate into successful performance in high technology products? According to a comprehensive analysis on the Italian system of innovation during the 1980s and the 1990s (Malerba, 1991), a full understanding of this matter has to start from the recognition that not one, but two innovation systems are present in Italy: a small firms network and a core R&D system. These two systems are quite different in terms of capabilities, organization and performance. The small firms network is composed of a large population of small and medium size firms (in some cases located in industrial districts), which interact intensively at the local level.

The core R&D system is composed of large firms with industrial laboratories, small high technology firms, universities, large public research institutes and the national government, linked through a complex organizational system at the national level.

The small firms network, grown up historically on a local, regional and vocational basis and characterized by capabilities accumulated through productive experience, has worked effectively and performed successfully during the past decades up until now. Firms in the network are engaged in rapid adoption of technology generated externally and in the adaptation and continuous improvement of this technology. The success of the system is based on the close interaction of a large number of firms bound to each other by economic, local, cultural and social factors. Firms incrementally innovate through learning by doing, by using and by interacting with suppliers and users.

The core R&D system, instead, much more recent than the small firms network and developed at a much later stage than those of countries such as Germany, the United Kingdom, France and the United States, is not characterized by advanced technological capabilities and does not perform satisfactorily in terms of innovation and international competitiveness. In Italy, in spite of a relevant quantitative growth of R&D during the 1980s, some of the qualitative elements needed for an effective and successful working of such a complex system are still missing or are not fully developed. In fact, first, several industries actors do not have advanced research and technological capabilities. Second, public policy for R&D support still exhibits major flaws. Third, an advanced national infrastructure of services for R&D and an overall coordination of public policies is still lacking. Fourth, advanced basic research performed in universities and public research centers is very unevenly distributed across institutions. Fifth, shortages of skilled scientists and engineers are present. Finally, there is no tradition of successful industry-university cooperation in research.

Table 1

Total R&D expenses as percentage of GDP, 1971-1992

	1971	1976	1981	1986	1991	1992
USA	2.46a	2.30	2.45	2.91	2.75	2.74
UK	2.10a	2.17b	2.41	2.34	2.08	2.00
France	1.88	1.75	1.97	2.23	2.42	2.36
Germany	2.20	2.16	2.43	2.73	2.66	2.58
Italy	***0.85***	***0.77***	***0.87***	***1.13***	***1.32***	***1.38***
Sweden	1.49	1.79b	2.30	2.89c	2.90	2.90
Japan	1.71	1.80	2.13	2.56	3.05	3.00
	a:1972	b:1975		c:1985		

Source: OCDE, 1994

2. Military R&D Activity

If we apply what is mentioned above to the military sector, we can see that adequate financial resources for R&D are available only within the major industrial military groups, which are often less efficient in performing innovative activities. As in the civilian sector, there is too little room (and funding) for small high-tech firms which are, on the contrary, more flexible than larger ones and able to implement innovations in a more efficient way.

In terms of GDP the level of R&D investments continues to remain low, and R&D funding is concentrated mainly in less advanced sectors without an effective coordination between research institutions and firms. Besides, the share of military R&D of total public R&D spending is high with respect to more dynamic countries like Germany or Japan, and low with respect to more similar industrial countries such as France or UK (see table 2).

Finally, in the international context Italy seems to have com-

Table 2
Military R&D as a share of total public R&D

	1986	1987	1988	1989	1990	1991	1992
USA	69.4	68.6	67.8	65.4	62.6	59.7	58.6
UK	49.3	45.5	42.7	43.6	42.5	44.8	45.2
France	34.0	35.9	37.3	37.0	40.0	36.1	34.6
Germany	12.1	12.7	12.4	12.8	13.5	11.0	10.5
Italy	***8.5***	***7.0***	***10.2***	***10.3***	***6.1***	***7.9***	***7.1***
Japan	4.1	4.5	4.8	5.1	5.5	5.7	5.9

Source: OCDE, 1994

petitive advantages only in traditional sectors, such as household appliances, or in sectors characterized by significant "learning by doing", such as industrial machines. In the military related sectors data provided by patents analysis stress a relevant weakness in areas such as missiles, aircraft, ships, communication equipments (see table 3).

3. Military R&D Funding

In Italy military R&D is financed by the Ministry of Defence budget; the National Applied Research Fund (law 46/1982); the national Fund for Technological Research (law 46/1982); the Ministry of Industry Fund for the Aerospace Sector (law 808/1985); the National Research Council (CNR), mainly through the socalled "Finalized Programs"; military firms (especially public owned ones).

In the Ministry of Defence budget there are at least four main items in which it is possible to find financial resources for R&D:

- item 7010 is specifically devoted to scientific research, but also items regarding weapon systems acquisition include a

Table 3
Index of technological specialization of advanced countries in military-related SIC classes

		USA	UK	F	D	SW	I
Guided Missiles and	(1)	1.23	1.77	1.77	1.03	1.22	0.21
Space vehicles	(2)	1.21	1.41	1.82	1.00	1.64	0.19
Ship, boat building	(1)	1.05	1.10	1.32	0.66	2.30	0.70
	(2)	1.09	1.14	1.54	0.69	1.62	0.43
Ordnance	(1)	1.12	0.65	1.21	1.41	2.69	1.10
	(2)	1.14	0.58	1.22	1.41	3.19	0.70
Aircraft and parts	(1)	0.84	1.46	1.39	1.32	0.85	0.87
	(2)	0.74	1.39	1.54	1.70	0.79	1.12

(1) Patent granted by the US Patent Office
(2) Patent citations, 1975-1988
Source: Pianta, Archibugi, 1991

relevant share of R&D;

- items 4011, 4031 and 4051 refer to military procurement for Army, Navy and Air Force, but include also expenses for research, development, industrialization, acquisition and maintainance of weapon systems, which means a large amount of military R&D (see table 4).

As regards the public resources assigned to defence as national goal, the following table shows that the Italian governement is spending about 10% of total R&D outlays for military R&D. Thus, Defence is the main goal pursued by the Italian government in the R&D sector outside universities. It is important to point out that the largest share of this amount is devoted to industrial R&D.

Finally, table 6 shows a relevant interest of the Ministry of Defence in financing technological research, but also its com-

Table 4

Ministry of Defence R&D expenditure 1987-1993 (billion lire, current price)

Year	Item 7010 (Scientific Research)	Scientific Research Expenditure in Other Items: Item 4004	Item 4011	Item 4031	Item 4051	Total
1987	53.8	0.2	158.6	101.0	178.0	491.6
1988	94.3	2.1	329.3	242.3	207.0	875.0
1989	130.0	0	158.2	33.0	49.4	340.6
1990	303.2	0	1,610.0	1,208.2	1,918.2	5,039.6
1991	292.0	0	70.4	56.4	98.0	516.8
1992	336.2	0	87.0	121.1	607.4	1,151.7
1993	410.4	0	26.2	101.6	656.1	1,194.2

Source: Ministry of Defence Budget Appropriations, various years

Table 5

Government R&D outlays for social-economic goals

	1988	1991
Ground environment	1.8%	1.4%
Ground protection	0.9%	0.4%
Environmental pollution	2.1%	3.0%
Human health	6.4%	6.5%
Energy	9.3%	5.4%
Agriculture	2.9%	3.3%
Industry	5.6%	7.2%
Defence	12.0%	8.4%
Total research activities within universities	36.8%	33.4%

Source: Ministry of Defence Budget Appropriations, 1993

Table 6
Sectors of R&D spending of Italian government and Ministry of Defence (million lire, current price 1991)

Sectors	Ministry of Defence	Total government spending
Mathematics	2,203	2,203
Physics	267	7,592
Chemistry	1,749	2,229
Technological research	743,989	787,899
Nuclear research	2,270	2,270
Space research	84,000	786,923
Interdisciplinary research	17,700	1,109,002
Others		526,923
Total	852,178	3,225,041

Source: IEFE, 1991

mitment in sustaining research activities in mathematics, chemistry and nuclear energy. Additionally, it is worth noting that the Ministry of Defence is the largest customer of manufacturing industry within the public sector.

4. Military R&D Organization

The Ministry of Defence is directly responsible for all military R&D activities in Italy. Within the Ministry of Defence, the Joint Chief of Staff defines, together with the Chiefs of Staff of the three Armed Forces, the guidelines of Defence R&D and military procurement.

The Defence Technical and Scientific Council (CTSD) is the advisory body of the Joint Chief of Staff in this field. A major role is played by the General Secretary of the Ministry of Defence (the highest technical and financial official of the Ministry), who represents the Italian Armed forces within the NATO-CNAD group as National Armaments Director. The General Secretary leads the technical branch of the Defence and is in charge of the definition of technical and commercial relations between the Ministry of Defence and industrial firms.

The Italian Ministry of Defence defines military R&D as those activities which, using state of the art technologies and the findings of technological research, can produce equipment to answer to specific operational needs. Thus, the process of developing a new equipment or system involves:

- the Minister of Defence (indirectly the Cabinet as a whole) at a political level;
- the Joint Chief of Staff, together with the three Chiefs of Staff, at a command level;
- the General Secretary-National Armaments Director, responsible for defining R&D programs, reducing duplications, evaluating programs, managing relations with industrial firms and foreign partners, at a coordination level;
- the Defence Technical and Scientific Council and the Defence-Industry Committee as advisory bodies at a consulting level;
- the Branch Offices, as operational bodies, at a management level;
- the Organizations which carry out research activities, at an executive level.

Military R&D is currently carried out by three main groups of organizations: research organizations of the Ministry of Defence, private and public military firms, universities and other research centers. However, Italian military research centers are very few. CRESAM (Center for Research and Studies for Military Purposes), located in Pisa, is the most important research center of the Italian Defence, and is dealing with four major research fields (nuclear energy, opto-electronics, electro-magnetic compatibility, and diagnostics materials). Besides, there are some technical centers which depend on the Army, the Air Force and the Navy, such as the Air Force Air Division for Studies, Research and Experiments (DASRS), particularly relevant for its collaboration with the aerospace industry. Some experimental center and firing grounds, then, depend on the three Armed forces as well. The areas of Salto di Quirra (Sardinia) for naval experimental activities, and Nettuno for ground artillery are well known.

According to the Defence White Paper 1985 (last source available), in 1983 there were 1,227 employees involved in Defence R&D activities, of whom about 600 are classified as "researchers".

As already mentioned, in Italy the major performers of military R&D are military private and public owned firms. Anyway, a general survey of the National Statistic Institute on R&D activities in the Italian industry, carried out in 1989, points out that investments of industrial firms in R&D military related activities can be considered relatively small, and that there are very few industrial groups totally involved in military production. More frequently firms produce both civilian and military products using the same technology. In this case the major part of investments for the development of gas turbines, ground vehicles and aircraft must be considered as civilian investments, while only investments for the development of new technologies in the armaments sector are totally devoted to military aims (see table 7). Unfortunately, as will be remarked in the concluding chapter, lacking a coherent R&D policy linked to the Ministry of Defence procuement policy, till now research activities carried out by individual firms have been driven only by medium term commercial tasks (such as to join an international program), without defining priorities resulting from wider policy choices.

5. Italian and EU Research and Technology Policy

In Italy the Ministry of University and Research publishes, every three years, a *Three Year Plan for Research* orienting national R&D activities towards some specific areas. In the 1994-1996 Plan ("Research and Innovation for Development") a section is devoted to defining, in a very general way, a military research policy. In this document there are two main aims strongly emphasized:

1. orienting research towards dual-use activities;
2. coordinating the Ministry of Defence military programs with other civilian research programs, mainly related to the so-called "diffusive technologies" (i.e. information technologies, biotechnologies and new materials).

With reference to the general aims of national policies in this

Table 7

Research personnel and research investment in industrial firms for selected military related sectors, 1989

Sector	Researchers	Technicians	Total personnel involved	Research investment (million lire)
Gas turbines, reactors	108	-	108	19,608
Nuclear reactors	122	50	218	26,381
Telecommunications device	5,214	3,440	10,218	1,041,982
Aerospace vehicles	2,008	1,460	4,118	969,753
Ground vehicles	1,526	3,140	9,317	1,272,734
Naval vehicles	110	156	289	46,681
Arms and ammunitions	368	359	966	73.933
Optics, fine mechanics	428	281	769	183,723
Total industrial sector	30, 520	21,301	64,944	8,698,468

Source: ISTAT, 1992

field, the Ministry of University and Research proposes to support five priority tasks of the Italian Armed forces: air defence; air deterrence, aeromobility, advanced training and C3I2 capabilities. To answer to such requirements it seems crucial, for the Italian Air forces, to acquire a national production capability in six weapon systems families:

- air defence systems (fighter aircraft, SAM missiles, ABM missiles, UAVs, etc.);
- air reconnaissance systems (satellites, aircraft, UAVs);
- transport aircraft;
- C3I2 systems;
- radar air defence systems (both airborne and ground-based);
- simulators for advanced training.

The main technological areas involved in these productions are: artificial intelligence, robotics, optoeletronics, composite materials, laser technology, radar technology.

As regards the Ministry of Defence technology policy, a forthcoming *Military Technology Plan* published by the Office of the Secretary General is expected to replace a 1989 document which listed 13 technological areas considered as a priority for the national defence. These technological areas were only partially related to technologies defined "critical" in both NATO and IEPG7 Euclid contexts. On the other hand, technologies which will be considered in the next Technology Plan (which are not available yet) are almost completely matched with technologies pursued within the WEAG/Euclid Program.

Finally, it is worth making a few remarks on the EU research policy. Promoting scientific research at European level is currently one of the main tasks of the EU. In the framework of the EU research policy, a lot of European programs are aimed at sustaining R&D projects dealing with new technologies carried out by small and medium firms. Considering only the programs acting in fields related to military activites (thus, potential conversion tools), we can list:

- Brite-Euram for promoting basic research on advanced materials, technologies for aeronautical safety, industrial innovation;
- Craft for funding external R&D activities (for small and medium firms without research facilities);
- Esprit for strengthening the European competition in microelectronics, system engineering in electronics, multimedia technologies, sensors and robotics, artificial intelligence);
- Race for projects on communication system integration;
- Joule and Thermie for energy saving.

In this context, a particular role could be played by the Sprint program, which is aimed at promoting technology transfer within the EU between research centers and other bodies. Even though conceived for technology transfer between civilian sectors, Sprint could be an important actor to promote a transfer of industrial and technological competence from military to civilian sectors.

6. Problems of Military R&D in Italy

Concluding this brief overview on the Italian military R&D, it must be emphasized that the R&D activity carried out within the Armed Forces and the Ministry of Defence research centers is very limited if compared to other European NATO countries. This implies two important consequences: a) the military R&D activity is highly concentrated within military firms, and, consequently, activities related to product development or applied research, which have more immediate economic results, are preferred to base research; b) a clear definition of the defence technological priorities is still missing.

On the one hand, the Italian Defence has systematically shown a strong dependence on US-NATO technological choices and on the industrial capacity of domestic defence industrial base; on the other hand, military firms have preferred to acquire foreign technology rather than to invest in research activity, thus remaining at a medium-low technological level.

Lacking a coordinated national industrial and technological policy - in the military sector as well as in the civilian one - military firms have been free to define their own strategic priorities, often supplying the Italian Defence with no "state of the art" equipment. In fact, the Italian military procurement can be defined as a "relief procurement", aimed at maintaining national industrial capacity in some military sectors without considering technological innovation and market competition. Actually the fall of Italian arms exports, experienced in the last years, can be widely explained by the patterns of Industry-Defence relationship.

A low level of activity in military R&D cannot bring to relevant spin-offs in civilian sectors (neither within the Ministry of Defence, nor within military firms). Thus, in Italy there are no public or private programmes for spreading military technologies. In the military industry a key issue is currently the development of dual-use equipments (or, with less emphasis, of dual use technologies). As already expalined, in Italy there are many military firms producing either for the civilian and the military sector, but they supply in both cases the same customer: the Italian State. Thus, a major issue in the Italian debate on conversion is "how to make military firms more efficient and competitive", no matter whether in military or civilian activities. Effectively, conversion is strictly linked to an increasing capacity of competing in open markets.

In this regard, it is maybe worth remembering that when the EU Commission decided in 1991 to establish European initiative to support national conversion activities, great expectations grew in Italy for this possibility to charge the Commission with the definition of national conversion policies (and of part of its financial burden). So, in the first phase of the Konver program the Italian government asked the Regions to prepare some proposals for conversion initiatives to be selected by the Ministry of Industry. The final result was a collection of industrial projects with no coherent national or regional strategy, highly criticized by the Commission for being too focused on an industrial policy perspective rather than on a regional one. Actually, Konver is not an industrial recovery program, but it is specifically oriented to support regional policies of conversion/diversification. Thus, the Ministry of Industry has substantially modified its approach to conversion policies, in order to put into action the 1993 phase of Konver and to regulate the future implementation of the manistream 1994-1999 Konver program. Currently, EU co-financed activities to support conversion include: assistance to newly established companies employing workers dismissed by military firms, funds to military laboratories and research centers to shift their military activities towards civilian fields, financial support for military firms diversification, and retraining activities for workers dismissed by military firms.

7. Conclusions

From this brief overview of the structure and competitiveness of the Italian innovation system, it is possible to draft some suggestions, also in order to face the problem of how to absorb technological and industrial capabilities coming from eventual reductions in military programs.

First, *the role of small/medium size firms should be emphasized.* It is really important, in areas affected by lagging of economic development or decline of traditional industries, to create a number of small companies acting in different sectors, with the aim of developing an "entrepreneural" culture and spreading technological know-how. A basic reason to support this type of approach is avoiding the economic waste often related to large recovery initiatives, such as large public financed programs carried out by military firms. On the contrary, it is important to sustain market oriented activites with *ad hoc* measures, that is to say providing industrial infrastructures, banking assistance, legal and tax consultancy, technical training and marketing services. In some countries, local governments created socalled "firms incubators" which have the task to support the creation of new companies. A network of these centers - Business Innovation Centers (BIC) - is currently sponsored by the EU.

Small and medium size firms cannot only manage business in providing services or in producing handicraft: evidence show that in Italy small innovative firms can play a key role in spreading science-based knowledges (including military technologies) and carrying out an industrial, especially high-tech, activity. A national policy of technology transfer can support this process creating joint ventures between large high-tech public owned firms, universities, research centers and small innovative firms. Some Italian laws are currently financing these activities, and local governments are fostering the creation of "scientific and technological parks", partially financed by the national government and the EU, aimed at developing science-based industrial productions.

Second, *different public policies should be coordinated more efficiently*. A frequent obstacle to the implementation of economic development policies is the difficulty in matching a wide range of goals. As an example, the task of transferring workforce and technologies from military aerospace large firms to a number of locally spread small firms should be analysed not only considering the technical and economic feasibility of such a move, but also general concerns regarding national policies in fields such as defence, technology, national economy, industry, trade, labour, etc. Thus, an agreement aimed at transferring a military technology from military firms to the commercial sector could be jeopardized if the Ministry of Defence considers that technology as strategic. Or a national policy of support to some industries could crowd out local investments for exploiting regional potential in terms of resources and technolgies. This means that an institutional framework within an industrial recovery plan should always be developed. In this context, EU general regulations must be considered as the general framework of all industrial policies.

Third, *industrial and technological policy should be matched together.* A characteristic of the Italian situation is the spreading of decision-making procedures related to military industrial activities over a lot of ministries. The Ministry of Industry is responsible for industrial policy decisions, the Ministries of Foreign Affairs and Foreign Trade control arms exports, the Ministry of Scientific Research coordinates research activities, and so on. It should be important, instead, to coordinate different national and EU policies, offering to military firms (which are often the only Italian firms in high-tech sectors) a clear perspective on: Armed Forces and social needs, export opportunities, scientific and technological national priorities, civilian and military procurement policies, industrial, economic and employment policies.

Fourth, *investments on dual use technologies should be increased.* Since the Italian military system cannot be present in all arms industry sectors, it is vital to concentrate industrial resources according to national defence priorities and to international collaborations, on those areas in which we have competitive advantages, such as ATC radars, trainer aircraft, AFVs, etc.).

In these fields the Ministry of Defence could sustain R&D with special interest in developing dual use technologies. Obviously, if it was possible to produce a large share of civilian production using the same technologies (civilian ATC systems, airframes, tractors, etc.) the Ministry of Defence commitment to acquire large amounts of military equipment, in order to finance military industrial activity, would be reduced.

Finally, it is necessary for the Ministry of Defence, facing shrinking budgets, to identify its needs in a more accurate way. In fact, *a more selective procurement policy* would lead to a wide process of restructuring military R&D and production system. In this context, the number of military firms would probably diminish, and the remaining ones would have to increase their presence in competitive civilian markets.[1]

1 The authors wish to thank Dr. Marcello Alessi for his precious help.

REFERENCES

1. AAVV (1986), *Rapporto sulla situazione e sulle prospettive della scienza in Italia,* Ist. Poligrafico e Zecca dello Stato, Rome.
2. AMENDOLA G:, PERRUCCI A. (1990), "La competitività dell'Italia nelle industrie high-tech: un approccio per prodotti", L'industria, XI, 2.
3. ANNUNZIATO P. (1992), *La capacità innovativa delle imprese,* XIV Rapporto CSC sull'Industria italiana, Roma.
4. ARCHIBUGI D., EVANGELISTA R., PIANTA M. (1992), "Il sistema innovativo italiano:punti di forza e di debolezza", paper presented to the Conference "Ritardo tecnologico e integrazione europea", Cnr, Rome, 16 December 1992.
5. BISOGNO P. (1986), "Politica della tecnologia e sicurezza", in JEAN C., *Sicurezza e difesa,* Angeli, Milan.
6. BOITANI A., CICIOTTI E. (1992), *Innovazione e competitività nell'industria italiana,* Il Mulino, Bologna.
7. CENTRO MILITARE DI STUDI STRATEGICI (1990), *L'organizzazione della ricerca e sviluppo nell'ambito difesa,* Rivista Militare, Rome.
8. CENTRO STUDI CONFINDUSTRIA (1992), XIV Rapporto CSC sull'industria italiana, May 1992.
9. COMMITTERI M., ROSSI S. (1992), "Tecnologia e competizione nel mercato unico europeo", paper presented to the Conference on "Ritardo tecnologico e integrazione europea, Cnr, Rome, 16 December 1992.
10. IEFE (1991), "Per una politica degli usi produttivi della tecnologia in Italia", *Economia e Politica Industriale,* 70.
11. ISTAT (1991), *Indagine statistica sull'innovazione tecnologica nell'industria italiana,* Rome.
12. MALERBA F. (1991), *Italy, the National System of Innovation,* CESPRI, Working Paper n.45, June.
13. MURST (1993), *Piano triennale della ricerca scientifica e tecnologica in Italia,* Istituto Poligrafico e Zecca dello Stato, Rome.
14. OECD (1991), *Choosing priorities in science and technology,* Paris.
15. OECD (1992), *Technology and the economy: the key relationships,* Paris.
16. OECD (1993), *Science and technology policy outlook,* Paris.
17. OECD (1994), *Main science and technology indicators,* Paris.
18. ONIDA F., MALERBA F. (1990), *La ricerca scientifica,* SIPI, Rome.
19. OFFICE OF TECHNOLOGY ASSESSMENT (1992), *Defence conversion. Redirecting R&D,* Congress of the United States, Washington.
20. PERANI G. (ed., 1992), *Ambienti per l'industria italiana,* ENEA, Rome.
21. PERANI G., PIANTA M. (1992), "The slow restructuring of the Italian arms industry", in BRZOSKA M., LOCK M., *Restructuring of arms production in*

Western Europe, SIPRI, Oxford University Press.

22. PIANTA M. (1988), "I programmi a tecnologia avanzata: ricerca militare o innovazione per l'economia?", *Economia e politica industriale*, 57.
23. PIANTA M., ARCHIBUGI D. (1992), *The technological specialization in advanced countries*, Kluwer Academic Publishers, Dordrecht.
24. PIANTA M., ARCHIBUGI D. (1992), "Convergenza e specializzazione delle attività innovative", paper presented to the conference "Ritardo tecnologico e integrazione europea, Cnr, Rome, 16 December 1992.
25. SPINARDI G. (1992), "Defence technology enterprises: a case study in technology transfer", *Science and Public Policy*, 19.
26. STEVENS G. (1991), "Les industries stratégiques dans les années 90", *L'observateuer de l'Ocde*, 172.

8

Military Conversion: a View from Brussels

Manfredo Macioti

The ending of the cold war and the beginning of a new paradigm in the relations between East and West may be taken to have begun five years ago, with the dismantling of the Berlin Wall. Cuts in defence spending and a process of economic adjustment have been in progress since that time. It has not been an easy transition, as the economies of the East have been severely retrenching over the past few years, while the West has gone through a phase of recession or, at best, sluggish growth. Unemployment has been and continues to be a great problem in both Regions.

Military Research and Defence Budgets

Government-funded R&D has an important part to play in a conversion strategy, as it is Government spending that has dominated defence research. There are seven countries in the OECD area whose Governments invest more than 10% of total Government outlays for R&D (1992) in military research and development. These are the USA (58.6%), the UK (45.2%), France (34.6%), Sweden (24.5%), Switzerland (18.5%), Spain (14.6%) and Germany (10.5%).

In the USA, defence-related R&D investment was in 1992 of the order of 44 b. $ (N.S.F. Science and Engineering Indicators, 1993). The Member States of the European Union (E.U.) invested about 11 b. ECU in defence R&D in 1990 (E.U. European Report on Science and Technology Indicators, 1994).

Data for military R&D in the former Soviet Union (FSU) are more difficult to obtain, but estimates put the figure at over 60% of total R&D in the 1980s and it probably still is nearly 50% of the total today. Russian R&D expenditure alone has been estimated at 140 b. Roubles in 1992 (perhaps equivalent to 1 b. $ at the time). However, there has been a dramatic reduction in funds for both civilian and defence research since 1991 virtually throughout the whole of the FSU.

Of the dozen or so other countries active in military science and technology in the world, it is probably China and India (with a reservoir of respectively 400,000 and 100,000 research scientists and engineers - RSE) which have the largest military-related research programmes. Japan - which has a larger research reservoir = 520,000 RSE - devotes a limited percentage of Government outlays (5.9%) to military expenditure. Thus the Japanese budget for military R&D barely exceeds the Swedish one.

Government statistics from India indicate that about 20% of national R&D expenditure is defence-related (S&T Data Book, 1991).

Direct employment in the E.U. armaments industry amounted to about 660,000 jobs in 1992. The peak level was reached in 1984, with a total of over 1 m. jobs (STOA, European Armaments Industry, Nov. 1993). Since then, employment has been steadily decreasing. Further cutbacks in defence budgets will further reduce this pool of specialized manpower by 150,000 to 200,000 individuals by the year 1996. In 1992, the military budget of the Twelve (E.U.) was 117 b. ECU, while the figure for the USA was 222 b. ECU. E.U. defence - related expenditure had decreased by 4.2% between 1989 and 1992, while the US decrease over the same period was nearly 10%. Not so Japan, whose military expenditure increased by 8.6% (from 22 b. ECU in 1989 to 23.9 b. in 1992).

Conversion

Generally speaking, in the E.U., the principle upheld by the Governments for many years that military research takes precedence over civilian research, is gradually giving way to the concept that there is a common denominator in military and civilian technologies, at the level of basic or generic research (*e.g.* in such fields as mathematics, aerodynamics, propulsion, semiconductors, etc.).

At the initiative of the European Parliament, the E.U. launched at the end of 1990 a special action, PERIFRA (Peripheral Regions and Fragile Activities), with a budget of 90 m. ECU, including some 56 m. ECU allocated to projects connected with the reduction of military expenditure. Another similar programme, KONVER, launched in 1993 with 130 m. ECU will assist the conversion of regions of the E.U. which are dependent on declining military activities. Over the years 1994-7, KONVER II should have a budget of 500 m. ECU.

As the monies available for defence-related expenditure continue to diminish in Europe, it is to be expected that the well established tradition in the field of military ventures at the European level (*e.g.* Jaguar, Alphajet, Tornado, E.F.A....) will receive a new impetus.

European cooperation is also due to grow in military research, where the European Independent Programme Group launched the European Cooperative Long Term Initiative in Defence (EUCLID) in 1988. This cooperation has been since 1993 entrusted to the Western European Armaments Group of the WEU.

Note should be taken of the fact that some of the E.U. own research programmes - such as ESPRIT, RACE, BRITE - partly cover research in technological fields which are of potentially "dual use". The share of "dual use" increases as we move from "Industrial Technologies and Materials" to "Information Technologies".

E.U./FSU Cooperation

The E.U. programme of technical assistance to the Commonwealth of independent States (TACIS), was launched in 1991 with the aim of speeding up the process of economic reform and transition to democracy underway in the FSU. The TACIS budget for 1994 is 510 m. ECU, the projects supported are mainly in the areas of human resources development, energy, nuclear safety, food production and distribution, transport, telecommunications and company services. Conversion projects were first included in 1993 and a total of 13 m. ECU has been invested so far by the E.U. in this area.

In 1992 the EU launched the International Association for the promotion of cooperation with scientists in the New Independent States of the FSU (INTAS). The emphasis of INTAS' action is on joint research programmes, involving laboratories in Western Europe and in the FSU. INTAS has 18 Members in the West (including the E.U.) and twelve partners in the East.

At about the same time, an initiative was launched at international level to help redirect the skills of highly qualified military researchers in the FSU toward civilian scientific projects. The International Science and Technology Centre (ISTC) opened its doors in Moscow earlier this year. It is funded by the E.U., the US, Japan and Russia. Several countries have joined the ISTC since, among them Armenia, Georgia, Belarus and Kazakhstan. It is projected that 4,000 to 5,000 scientists will eventually be involved.

Another useful link between the E.U. and the FSU is the TEMPUS programme, devoted since 1993 to strengthening relations in higher education between Western Europe, Russia, Ukraine and Belarus. Since the current academic year 1994/5, four other Republics (Kazakhstan, Kyrghyzstan, Moldova and Uzbekistan) have been participating in the TEMPUS programme. It is foreseen that three more FSU States (Armenia, Azerbaijan and Georgia) as well as Mongolia will join in 1995/96.

The Examples of Belarus and Ukraine

Belarus. As part of the FSU, Belarus started a programme for the conversion of military production as early as 1989. The programme required each defence-related enterprise to embark upon the production of civil products. Most enterprises "converted" by simply producing what was easiest for them from an engineering and technical point of view, without preliminary investigations in the potential markets. As a consequence, effective progress in conversion has been limited (TACIS, Contract Information 1993, January 1994).

Belarus has about 5% of the former Soviet defence-industrial base. The military industry of Belarus consists of some 120 major establishments employing about 400,000 workers (including research institutes with 20,000 staff). The current decline in demand has heavily affected the sector. It is estimated that military enterprises in Belarus are working at some 20% of their nominal capacity. On the positive side, the defence industry has been employing highly qualified people at senior level, and well skilled staff for design, research and manufacturing activities. There are accordingly in Belarus valuable human and physical resources available for conversion. This is particularly true in such areas as radio and telecommunications, optical system, electronics and military transport technology.

The TACIS assistance for the conversion of Byelorussian defence industry for 1993 totals 1.7 m. ECU and consists of actions in the areas of telecommunications equipment (Agat, Gomel, Luch, Zenit, Lös, Cri...) and optical products (Belomo).

Ukraine. Ukraine has roughly between 15 and 30% of the former Soviet defence plants and military R&D facilities. There are in particular some 700 plants with 500,000 employees directly active in defence industries, and perhaps another 1 m. people contributing to defence output. Within the FSU, Ukraine is the second largest producer of weapons and military equipment after Russia. Ukraine is capable of assembling all major categories of such equipment (ships, missiles, transport aircraft, land arms and radars). Some Ukraine facilities have unique capabilities: thus Ukraine has the only shipyard in the FSU currently capable of building aircraft carriers (CIA, The Defence Industries of the Newly Independent States of Eurasia, January 1993).

The defence sector is at present confronted with a sharp drop in demand for military equipment and components, but the great majority of the employees are still on the pay-roll. The Ukrainian Government has established an ambitious programme for the conversion of more than 500 military enterprises. Funds have been earmarked at the level of the new Ministry of Engineering, Military-Industrial Complex and Conversion, to foster the conversion programme. First priority is given to the production of medical and agricultural equipment, as well as to the production of equipment for the energy sector (TACIS Contract Information 1993, January 1994).

TACIS will, under the 1993 conversion programme, provide 2.85 m. ECU to assist the following three projects:

- development by Hartron in Kharkov of two high-tech control systems in the field of energy;
- conversion by two enterprises in Kiev (Relay & Automatic and the Electronic Instrumentation Research Institute) with a view to developing and manufacturing medical equipment;
- development of business relations with Western markets by the Donetsk Institute of Automation and two enterprises in Kiev (Elektroapparat and Monolit).

Furthermore, TACIS will assist the Ukrainian National Programme with 6.36 m. ECU for the retraining of military officers (and members of their families). This European effort complements the assistance that Germany has granted to Ukraine (DM 23 m. over the period 1991 to 1994) for the training and retraining of discharged military personnel and their families following their return from Germany to Ukraine.

Conclusion

If we define defence conversion as the process by which skills, research, technology and equipment in the defence area are shifted into alternative economic applications, then conversion is not an easy process to implement. Nevertheless dual-use approaches - technologies, processes and products with both military and commercial applications - can be developed in several areas of industry. This is particularly true at the lower levels of a vertical product hierarchy. Thus research may conveniently cover fields common to both areas. Examples range from composite materials to sensors, information science, modeling and simulation, robotics and artificial intelligence, telemedicine, fibre optics and photonics, laser systems, to acoustics and mathematics.

In any case, the success of a conversion policy is highly dependent on the general economic context and a sound legislative framework. A poorly developed banking system, hyperinflation, reluctant privatization efforts or legal uncertainties in such critical areas as trade, investment and industrial property rights, will neither favour real conversion, nor attract an appropriate level of international cooperation and investment.

Bibliography

Government of India (Department of Science and Technology)
Science and Technology, Pocket Data Book 1991
New Delhi, 1991

CIA (Directorate of Intelligence)
The Defence Industries of the Newly Independent States of Eurasia
Washington, January 1993

National Science Board (N.S.F.)
Science and Engineering Indicators
Washington, 1993

STOA (European Parliament)
European Armaments Industry: Research, Technological Development and Conversion
Luxembourg, November 1993

TACIS (European Commission)
Contract Information, Budget 1993
Brussels, January 1994

European Commission
The European Report on Science and Technology Indicators 1994
Luxembourg, 1994

9
Impact of Defense Conversion and US Response

Nicholas Montanarelli

In March 1993, President Clinton announced a conversion plan that would spend $20 billion over five years. Of that, $1.7 billion was spent in the remainder of fiscal year 1993. In fiscal year 1994, $3.3 billion would be obligated and by fiscal year 1997, funding would be increased to $5.3 billion per year. This money was to help people find new jobs, create technologies that have both civilian and military uses, and assist commercial technologies of national importance by using new methods such as information highways.[1]

Reacting to public concern over higher taxes, the U.S. Congress has reduced the funds to half of what was called for in 1994 and the outlook for the next few years will likely reflect these current reductions.

As a result of the end of the Cold War many members of Congress campaigned in 1992 with a call for 50 percent cuts in the defense budget. Ironically, they must now find ways to create jobs in states like California that will lose an estimated 650,000 defense related jobs. Many of us who are responsible for making defense conversion work are constantly reminded how difficult it is for a company to take new products into new markets. It is even harder for a defense company to be competitive in many commercial markets with the kind of overhead structures they have geared toward defense.

Many times it takes as long as 20 years of very patient efforts to make the conversion from military to civilian products. It is a generally accepted rule that conversion efforts take a long time and the probability of success is uncertain.

It is also difficult to measure the success of overall conversion efforts. While all the evidence is anecdotal, it seems to indicate that federal programs work slowly, at best. A number of small companies have successfully diversified already. But many of these firms have done so, thanks to strategic planning, a strong management commitment, and realism that it would be accomplished with little or no government funding. Many of the early conversion programs were seeking an elusive panacea to magically create jobs and produce products on a scale similar to the defense production that preceded it.

The U.S. defense industrial base faces a radical restructuring that will continue over the next several years. Concerns for deficit reduction by the general public will result in new domestic spending priorities. Not only is U.S. defense policy undergoing a major review of roles and missions in the post-Cold War era but within the armed forces, such basic concerns as force structure, U.S. basing, and overseas deployments are in flux.

The long-term downward trajectory of U.S. defense budgets has generated considerable uncertainty for both large and small companies doing business with the Department of Defense (DOD). The U.S. defense budget declined 29 percent between fiscal year 1985 and fiscal year 1993. Under the Clinton Administration proposed budget funding for national defense is projected to fall from $273 billion in fiscal year 1993 to $227 billion in 1997, a further 17 percent drop. Projections by the Electronics Industries Association (EIA) suggest that defense budgets could fall to around $215 billion by the turn of the century, while there have been calls in the U.S. Congress and elsewhere to reduce military funding to $180 billion by fiscal year 1997.[2]

The effects of funding changes, and their impact on both defense and industry will be described in brief scenario specific descriptions that we hope will effectively make the audience aware of the vast complexity of implementing the transition of what is referred to as defense conversion.

Meeting the Challenge with Federal Assistance

There are over 50 government programs funded to assist in defense conversions. We have focused on the three programs we feel will have the greatest impact on the U.S. economy.

The largest program is the Technology Reinvestment Project (TRP) whose mission is to stimulate the defense transitions to the high tech areas of the industrial complex. The TRP is managed for the DOD by the Advanced Research Project Agency (ARPA). It provides the most advanced, affordable military systems and the most competitive commercial products. The TRP's individual programs are structured to expand on high technology employment opportunities in industry that will demonstrably enhance U.S. competitiveness. This is being accomplished through the application of defense and commercial resources to develop dual-use technologies, manufacturing and technology assistance to large and small firms. Each enhance U.S. manufacturing skills and target displaced defense industry workers.[3]

In order to meet future demands for advanced technical weapons capability while the defense budget declines, the DOD, by direction of the U.S. Congress, budgeted $465 million in 1993 for the TRP. The funds were used to stimulate the transition of defense technology to a growing, integrated national industrial capability that provides the most advanced, affordable military systems and the most competitive commercial products. Over 212 projects were funded in the areas of technology development, technology deployment, and education and training in manufacturing.

Technology development programs were funded to accelerate the commercialization of the dual-use technologies that foster integration of the defense and commercial industrial bases. At the same time, they provide for the national defense by promoting cutting edge commercial and defense capabilities. Programs funded in the area of technology deployment assist new and established manufacturers in becoming globally competitive and achieving world class standards.

An added feature is the coordination of Federal, state, and local resources to improve and concentrate the flow of services to areas of opportunity. Education and training programs are intended to build a highly skilled manufacturing work force for the future. Defense engineers and technicians will be retrained so they can contribute to the commercial and defense industries of today.

All of the TRP programs mentioned have three common requirements. Each program is made through a competitive award; it must emphasize partnership, when possible; and to reduce risk, each award is cost-shared at least 50 percent.

The success of the first year of this program is indicated by White House and Congressional direction to budget $670 million for the 1994 TRP.

The second largest program is the Federal government to help offset the impact of defense conversion is the Advanced Technology Program (ATP). Begun in 1990, the ATP, located at the National Institute of Standards and Technology (NIST), promotes the economic growth and competitiveness of U.S. business and industry by accelerating the development and commercialization of promising, high-risk technologies with substantial potential for enhancing the U.S. economy. The program provides technology development funding on a cost-sharing basis through cooperative agreements to single businesses or industry-led joint ventures. In selecting broad programmatic areas, the ATP relies on its overall strategy of drawing on industry's ideas.

To date there have been four annual competitions with $515 million total funds committed ($247 - government; $268 - private). Eighty-nine awards have been made ranging from $500,000 to $20 million.

A good mixture of participants has resulted in 23 awards to

joint ventures and 66 to single applicants. The nature of the ATP has allowed for the entry of industries that are vital to continuing economic growth. These industries include biotech, energy, chemicals, electronics, computing, communications, and, very important, manufacturing. The success of this program so far has produced a strong market orientation that calls for an annual budget of $750 million by 1997.[4]

The current administration has put great faith in the role small business will play in helping the U.S. adapt to the economic slow down resulting from military base closings, and cutbacks in defense and aerospace.

NIST has been given a broad-base task to build a nationwide system of technology services for the nation's small manufacturers. The Manufacturing Extension Partnership (MEP) is designed to be a comprehensive, yet locally responsive network to help firms upgrade their equipment, improve their processes, and strengthen their business performance. The MEP, which is made up of Manufacturing Technology Centers (MTCs), state, and partnering organizations, will be an entry point into an integrated national system of technical resources, services, and expertise provided by the government.

The MEP builds on NIST's many years of experience in manufacturing extension and on productive partnerships forged with public and private organizations at the national, state, and local levels. Through the MEP, the Clinton Administration has set a goal of creating a nationwide network of 100 manufacturing centers by 1997.

Its mission can be simply stated; technology gaps will be resolved by using resources of improved manufacturing technology as required by small and midsize companies that need it. Center staff activities work with companies through one-on-one assistance and in groups organized around common needs, industries, or technologies.

The goal of the MEP centers is not to create jobs but rather to protect existing jobs. Results are measured through reduced costs, increased sales, improved productivity and product quality, enhanced customer satisfaction, and greater profits. As of September 1993 an estimated Federal investment of $54 million has had a bottom-line result of over $320 million in savings. In addition, the corresponding changes that firms make with MEP centers' assistance improve manufacturers' abilities to compete, to grow, and to sustain high wage, high quality jobs that strengthen the U.S. manufacturing base. By saving and improving current jobs in the manufacturing sector, we can sustain, to a certain degree, the impact of defense cuts.[5]

Issues and Needs of American Industry

The U.S. Department of Commerce is working with U.S. business to address issues resulting from defense conversion that will promote sustained economic growth, job creation, and a rising standard of living. To compensate for the continuing reduction in defense spending, changes in three major areas of technology policy are recommended. They are technology development, technology diffusion, and technology infrastructure.

To increase U.S. technology development, many industrial organizations urge increased financial support by the Federal government for generic research and development (R&D). This could be accomplished through increased funding for large government programs, such as the Advanced Technology Program and the Technology Reinvestment Project, and more support for manufacturing and process technologies. Individual states that are greatly impacted by defense cutbacks would like to have a bigger say in setting Federal research priorities. There is a general feeling by industry that if low-priority government programs that duplicate industry efforts to enter the market place are eliminated, there would be greater initiative to start new ventures. Government programs should facilitate precompetitive research and test-bed development. Federal support is ideally directed to particular research subjects including manufacturing and process technologies, best manufacturing practices, high performance computing and communications, environmental technology, and service sector technology.

Two main tax policy recommendations that could help industry are that the research and experimentation (R&E) tax credit be made permanent, and that whatever tax there is on capital gains be lowered relative to the tax on ordinary income. Tax credits for all R&E expenditures should be considered. Other incentives to stimulate industry cooperation would be providing a 10 percent credit for industry-sponsored university research; providing a special credit for companies engaged in collaborative R&D; and considering ways to improve the tax credits available to smaller firms.

In the area of technology diffusion, industry would like greater exposure to technology transfer.

In the 1980s, the U.S. Congress passed a number of laws focused on helping industry and universities to work closer with Federal R&D to meet the challenge of foreign competition. These laws are playing a major role in meeting the goals of defense conversion through technology diffusion. As a result, many organizations want more and are having more private sector involvement in Federal technology transfer, commercialization, development, and deployment policies.[6]

The Defense Department is currently giving the private sector more responsibility for maintaining defense equipment. In turn, this frees up vital military resources while creating jobs in many industrial sectors.

New Federal programs, discussed in a previous section, have been implemented to accelerate industrial modernization. Programs such as Cooperative Research and Development Agreements between government and industry are in the process of being streamlined, while government agencies with research laboratories are devoting more resources to marketing their technologies to the private sector. Several new national data bases are being formed to assist in this process.

What is needed is more attention to bridging the gap between the Federal laboratories and U.S. industry. There are several investigative panels looking into ways the Federal government may involve itself directly in the commercialization process, such as providing loans and equity, without becoming competitive to the venture capital and investment banking sectors that are vital to our economy.

Many advocate a variety of tax proposals to foster technology commercialization. Some of these proposals urge re-examination of current U.S. international tax policies in light of the fact that U.S. companies must increasingly compete in the global marketplace. Issues, such as ways to improve how foreign earned income is taxed and how royalties on intellectual property are realized, need to be readdressed.

Some organizations representing industry are pushing for new laws to support investment tax credit, more accelerated depreciation, and reforming our Alternative Minimum Tax which tends to reverse innovation incentives for certain taxpayers. Many groups are lobbying against any increase in the current corporate tax rate. They are asking for lower corporate tax rates in exchange for the elimination of generous write-offs.

There is a strong effort by this administration to increase the importance of manufacturing as an element of national policy. Many would like to see it as a main technological focus area such as those in defense, space, health, and energy.

If defense conversion is going to work, we need to make major improvements in government procurement. Some of the recommendations include letting industry use commercial practices; simplifying audits and oversight; and increasing the use of "best value" techniques to account for factors other than the lowest price. We should also create incentives for the use of advanced manufacturing technologies; removal of the bias against commercial products in defense procurement; and providing more multi-year procurement and budgeting.[7]

To meet the need to employ individuals affected by reductions in defense, major infrastructure changes, through an enhanced coordination of Federal education programs, must be made. Upgrades in achievement standard, raising math and science levels, curriculum changes, promoting team building, and more technical education are required. Better coordination of Federal education programs, increased prestige of the teaching profession, and experimental programs in different regions are helping to upgrade the work force. Additional programs, in new vocational categories where the jobs exist, are being funded by the government in areas affected by military base closings. Extensive support, in the form of tax incentives, is given to companies having employee stock ownership programs that let individuals deduct the cost of formal education and training for a new job.

Some industrial organizations (professional societies and trade associations) want the U.S. to rely on voluntary industry standards allowing more private sector input on a National Information Infrastructure (NII).

There is considerable support for strengthening intellectual property rights at home and abroad, including increased protection for software, and the property rights resulting from Federally funded technology (e.g., technology produced by industry-government cooperative agreements).

Recommendations on standards for U.S.-produced products vary. Industry would like to strengthen the U.S. system for getting U.S. standards accepted internationally.

Industry is on record to help do whatever is required to increase savings and investment, lower the budget deficit, and make more long-term, low-cost capital available for business.

Some specific measures are: create a consumption-based income tax; give added support to the consumer through individual retirement accounts and family-based saving plans; and place limits on the ability of the Federal Reserve to manipulate money supply growth, the Federal Funds rate, and the exchange rate.

Numerous organizations recommend integration of policies across the technology spectrum to include trade policy, monetary policy, regulatory policy, human resources policy, investment policy, fiscal policy, national security policy, and environmental policy.

Everyone you talk to would call for the Administration and Congress to support reform of product liability law. Current laws tend to discourage innovation and commercialization, and need to be amended to reflect the reality of global competition. A uniform Federal law on product liability to help meet, rather than frustrate, U.S. technology goals is long overdue.

While discussing product liability reform, we should not overlook the need for regulatory reform of antitrust laws for research, overseas marketing, and joint production. Much could be accomplished by having more reasonable interpretation of existing laws.

Conclusion

As we have stated in somewhat brief descriptions, the Federal government and U.S. Industry are making a considerable effort to transform how we do business today. In recent years, the government officials have sought new goals for their research dollars. One of the most important emerging themes in the Federal programs is international competitiveness. Large Federal expenditures are made to support R&D that will increase American productivity, thereby helping industry in global economic competition. This, in turn, will play a key role in absorbing a large quantity of resources affected by the end of the Cold War.

There are many who do not believe that a new competitiveness rationale will enhance the economy by reinvigorating the national R&D effort. These individuals believe that competitiveness is not a politically powerful substitute for the Cold War in forging a durable coalition for supporting R&D at the generous levels typical of the past decades. There are also those who believe that many of the new programs are shaped by political necessity and may likely undermine the economic performance of the programs when the political needs are shifted. In contrast, the current approach to R&D and its technology is essentially economy-wide. Its appeal rests on the argument that it can help U.S. industry boost productivity which will increase both its domestic and international markets. Almost every industrial sector has been a target for Federal support.

The new methods of technology enhancement taken by the government have caused two major changes to how Federal R&D programs are formulated and managed. One change is greater privatization in the selection and results of research projects. This has given private industry responsibility for technical choices in the projects and essentially all intellectual property rights. The other change has been increased collaboration among industry and research organizations.

To some degree, failures should be expected because the outcome of an R&D effort is inherently unpredictable. What we haven't learned thus far is how to analyze, and rapidly terminate government programs that are regarded as technical failures. Government officials, unlike industry managers, are more sensitive because of political pressure to the effects that canceling a project will have on employment. In short, the government has difficulty completing successful projects and difficulty in cutting its losses on failures.[8]

No matter what the outcome of government/industry technology development, we must believe that the possible benefits of a discovery can be realized only if people other than the discoverers have the opportunity and incentive to apply new findings to their needs. This will ultimately determine the success of our defense conversion program. In the meantime, the government can improve the performance of selected economic sectors by adopting policies that facilitate and increase investments in technology through research, development, and manufacturing.

NOTES

1 United States General Accounting Office, January 1994. "Defense Conversion; Slow Start Limits Spending" Washington, D.C. 20548 USA.

2 Bitzinger, Richard A. Defense Budget Project, April 1993, "Adjusting to The Defense Drawdown: The TransitionIn The Defense Industry" pages 3-4, Washington, D.C. 20002 USA.

3 Defense Technology Conversion, Reinvestment, and Transition Assistance, March 1993 Technology Reinvestment Project, page 1-1, Arlington, Virginia 22203-1714 USA.

4 Advance Technology Program, U.S. Department of Commerce, National Institute of Standards and Technology, Gaithersburg, Maryland 20899-0001 USA.

5 Manufacturing Extension Partnership, U.S. Department of Commerce, National Institute of Standards and Technology, March 1993, Gaithersburg, Maryland 20899-0001 USA.

6 Brown, Harold. Critical Issues in Defense Conversion, September 1993, The Center for Strategic & International Studies, pages 27-28, Washington, D.C. 20006 USA.

7 Listening to Industry: Business Views on Technology Policy, June 1994, pages 17-23, U.S. Department of Commerce, Technology Administration, Office of Technology Policy, Washington, D.C. 20230 USA

8 Cohen, Linda R. and Noll, Roger G. Privatizing Public Research, Scientific American, September 1994, pages 73-75, New York, New York 10017-1111 USA.

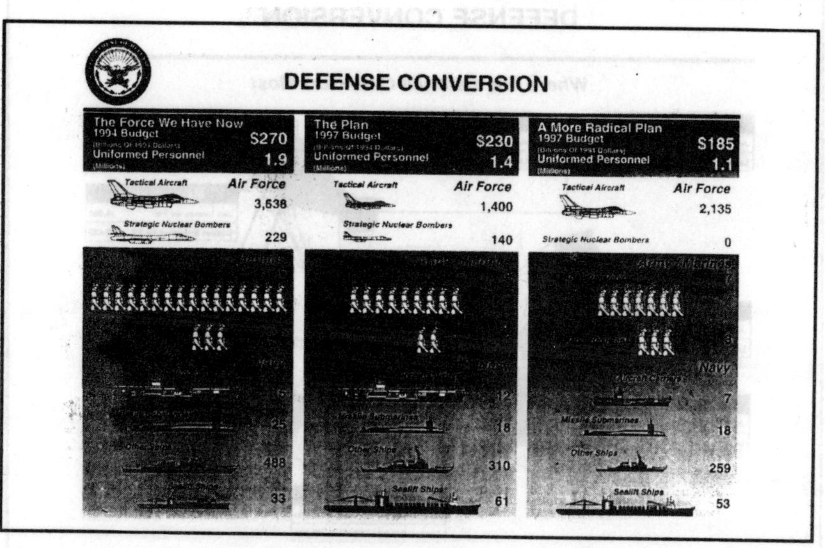
DEFENSE CONVERSION
The Force We Have Now
1994 Budget
$270
Uniformed Personnel
1.9
Tactical Aircraft
Air Force
3,638
Strategic Nuclear Bombers
229
488
33
The Plan
1997 Budget
$230
Uniformed Personnel
1.4
Tactical Aircraft
Air Force
1,400
Strategic Nuclear Bombers
140
12
Missile Submarines
18
Other Ships
310
Sealift Ships
61
A More Radical Plan
1997 Budget
$185
Uniformed Personnel
1.1
Tactical Aircraft
Air Force
2,135
Strategic Nuclear Bombers
0
Navy
7
Missile Submarines
18
Other Ships
259
Sealift Ships
53

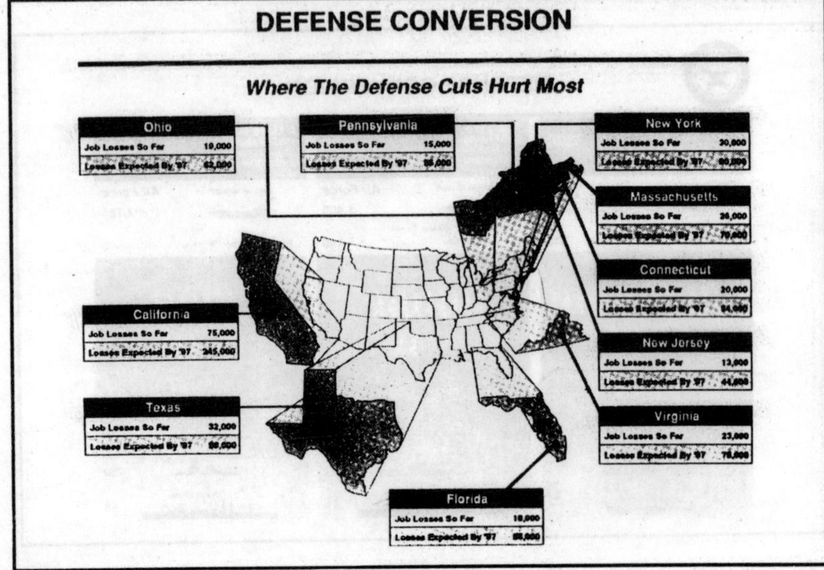

DEFENSE CONVERSION GOALS

- **Facilitate The Transition By Encouraging Economic Growth**
- **Preserve Defense Capability**
- **Ease The Immediate Impact On Workers, Communities And Companies**
- **Improve Government Programs (More Effective And Efficient)**

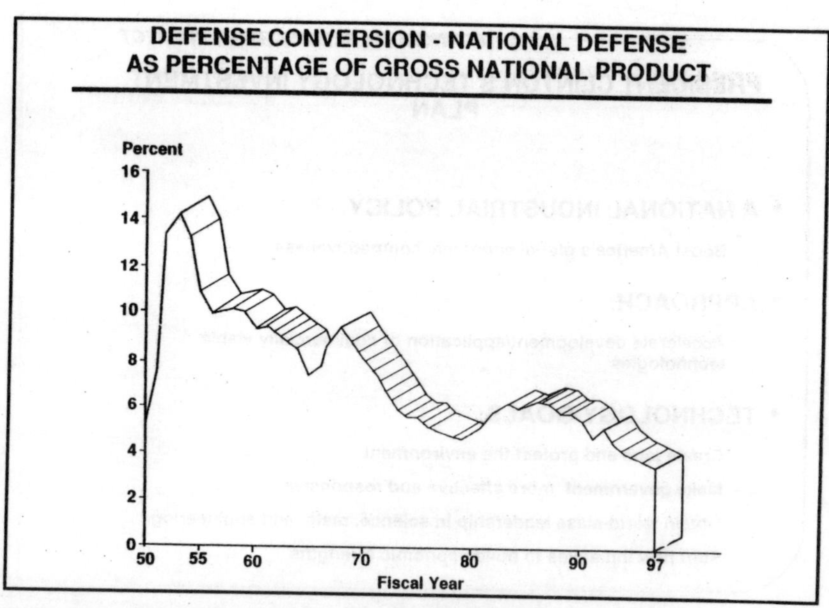
DEFENSE CONVERSION - NATIONAL DEFENSE
AS PERCENTAGE OF GROSS NATIONAL PRODUCT
Percent
16
14
12
10
8
6
4
2
0
50
55
60
70
80
90
97
Fiscal Year

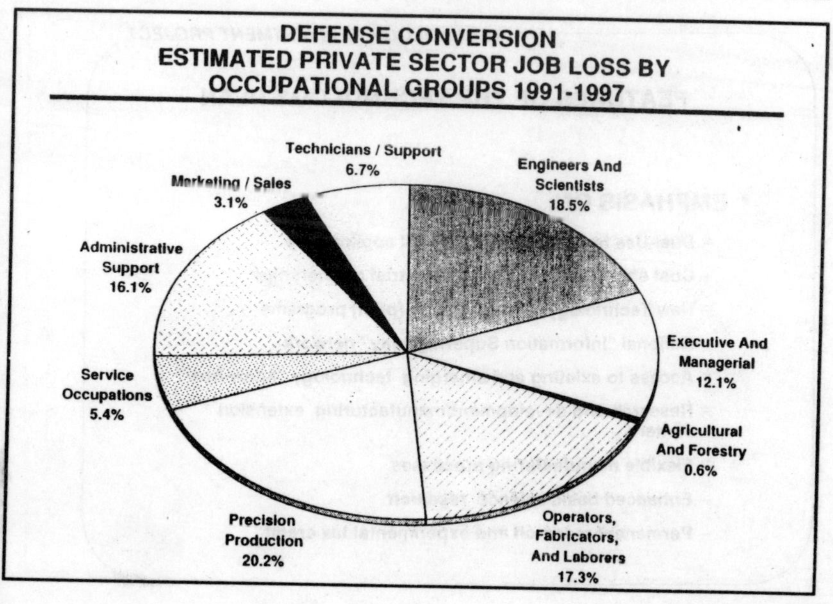
DEFENSE CONVERSION
ESTIMATED PRIVATE SECTOR JOB LOSS BY
OCCUPATIONAL GROUPS 1991-1997
Technicians / Support
6.7%
Engineers And
Scientists
18.5%
Marketing / Sales
3.1%
Administrative
Support
16.1%
Executive And
Managerial
12.1%
Service
Occupations
5.4%
Agricultural
And Forestry
0.6%
Precision
Production
20.2%
Operators,
Fabricators,
And Laborers
17.3%

TECHNOLOGY REINVESTMENT PROJECT

PRESIDENT CLINTON'S TECHNOLOGY INVESTMENT PLAN

- **A NATIONAL INDUSTRIAL POLICY:**
  - **Boost America's global economic competitiveness**
- **APPROACH:**
  - **Accelerate development/application of commercially viable technologies**
- **TECHNOLOGY GOALS:**
  - **Create jobs and protect the environment**
  - **Make government more effective and responsive**
  - **Obtain world-class leadership in science, math, and engineering**
  - **Start new initiatives to build economic strengths**

TECHNOLOGY REINVESTMENT PROJECT

FEATURES OF THE TECHNOLOGY PLAN

- **EMPHASIS ON:**
  - **Dual-Use technology commercial applications**
  - **Cost shared Government - industrial partnerships**
  - **New Technology Demonstration (pilot) programs**
  - **National "Information Superhighway" network**
  - **Access to existing and emerging technology "know-how"**
  - **Research and development/manufacturing extension canters**
  - **Flexible manufacturing processes**
  - **Enhanced basic science research**
  - **Permanent research and experimental tax credit**

BUZE WORDS

- Strategic Partnerships
- Dual Use Technology
- Defense Conversion
- Industrial Consortia
- Regional Alliances
- Manufacturing Technology
- Technology Transfer
- Technology Applications
- Technology Utilization
- Technology Transition
- Spin-offs

TECHNOLOGY REINVESTMENT PROJECT

TECHNOLOGY REINVESTMENT PROJECT

MISSION

To stimulate the transition to a growing, integrated, national industrial capability which provides the most advanced, affordable, military systems and the most competitive commercial products.

STRATEGY

Invest Defense Conversion, Title IV funds in activities which stimulate the:

1. ***Development*** **of technologies which enable new products and processes**
2. ***Deployment*** **of existing technology into commercial and military products and processes**
3. ***Integration*** **of military and commercial research and production activities**

1

TECHNOLOGY REINVESTMENT PROJECT

ACTIVITY AREAS

- **TECHNOLOGY DEVELOPMENT**
  Promote the development of dual-use technologies
  - ***Spin-Off Transitioning*** **(activities that demonstrate commercial viability and have already been developed for defense purposes)**
  - ***Dual-Use Development*** **(activities that are applicable to commercial and defense)**
  - ***Spin-On Promotion*** **(activities that demonstrate defense applicability and have already been developed for commercial purposes)**

- **TECHNOLOGY DEPLOYMENT**
  Establish links between existing technology capabilities for small and medium-sized businesses
  - ***Manufacturing Extension Service Providers*** **(outreach)**
  - ***Extension Enabling Services*** **(services to integrate service providers and technical sources)**
  - ***Alternative Deployment Pilot Projects*** **(in-reach)**
  - ***Technology Access Services*** **(brokering, "yellow pages," etc.)**

3

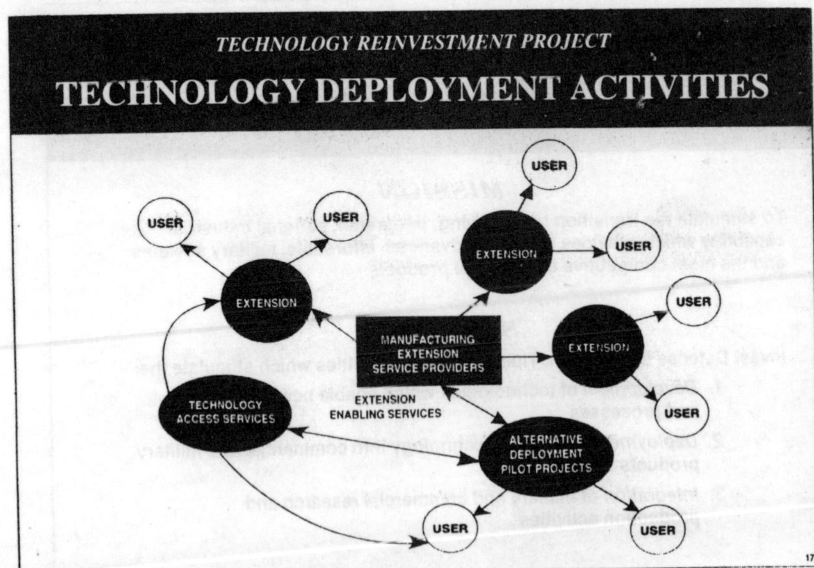

TECHNOLOGY REINVESTMENT PROJECT

ACTIVITY AREAS
(continued)

- **MANUFACTURING EDUCATION AND TRAINING**
  Establish programs for the retraining of defense workers and improve the manufacturing curriculum in the academic sector
  - **Engineering education in manufacturing across the curriculum**
  - **Practice-oriented master's degree programs**
  - **Educational traineeships for defense industry engineers**
  - **Manufacturing engineering education coalition**
  - **Supplementary education awards to ongoing centers and coalitions devoted to manufacturing**
  - **Individual/group innovations in manufacturing engineering education**

4

TECHNOLOGY REINVESTMENT PROJECT

COST SHARING

- **All programs have cost sharing (match) requirements at least 50%**
- **Match can include:**
  - ***Cash***
    - **Can come from participants or third parties**
    - **May include IR&D under some circumstances**
    - **Includes license fees, royalties, fees for services**
    - **SBIR Program**
  - ***In-kind Contributions***
    - **Compensated services of personnel**
    - **Value of equipment, land, buildings**
    - **Technology transfer activities**

5

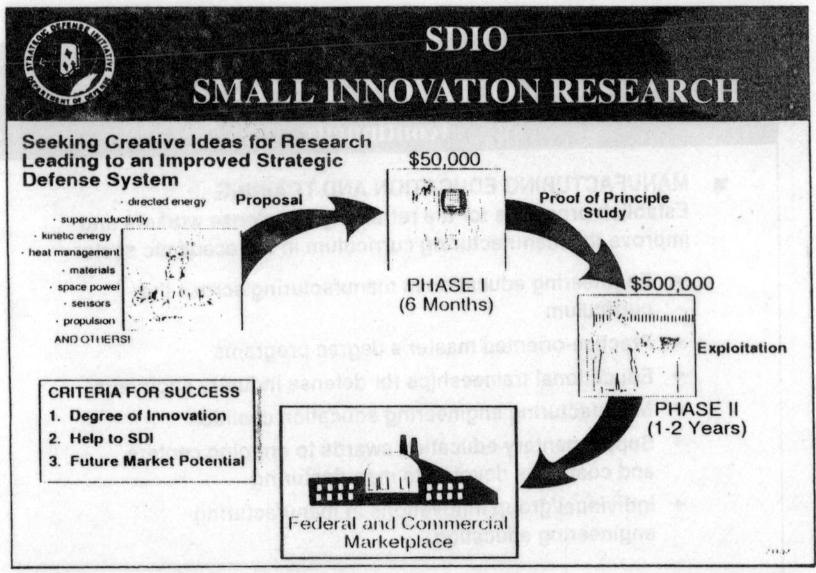

TECHNOLOGY REINVESTMENT PROJECT

INTELLECTUAL PROPERTY RIGHTS

- **GENERAL POLICY**
  - **Government to acquire nothing if technology commercialized in a reasonable time**
  - **Restrict foreign access to technology**
  - **Encourage broad exposure to technology among consortium partners**
- **PATENT RIGHTS**
  - **Contracts, grants, and cooperative agreements**
  - **"Other transactions"**
- **RIGHTS IN OTHER INTELLECTUAL PROPERTY**

8

Advanced Technology Program

MISSION

- **Stimulate U.S. economic growth through the development and application of high-risk technologies by companies**

ATP PROGRAM SELECTION

PURPOSE *IS* TO:

- **Define and implement high-risk, high payoff R&D programs**
- **Establish a framework for industry and government partnerships to develop national R&D programs**
- **Stimulate and facilitate public discussion and sharing of non-proprietary ideas for future technology and business directions**
- **Encourage industry to submit program ideas**

ATP PROGRAM DEFINITION

PURPOSE *IS NOT* TO:

- **Provide single companies or small groups of companies with a mechanism for funding research proposals that benefits only their companies and has little impact on the overall economy**
- **Force companies to cooperate with each other or with federal agencies or universities**
- **Provide federal assistance to carry out work that would otherwise be performed in a timely manner by the private sector**

MAJOR CHARACTERISTICS OF THE ATP

- **Development/application of high-risk technologies to stimulate economic growth**
- **Market oriented -- industry proposes ideas, shares costs, and performs work**
- **Competitive selection process -- technical and business merit**
- **Cost sharing**

ATP ELIGIBILITY

- Individual companies
  - No more than 3 years
  - Up to $2 million total
  - ATP pays only direct costs
- Joint ventures
  - No more than 5 years
  - No limit on award amount
  - ATP share less than 50%
- No direct funding to universities, government agencies or non-profit independent research institutes

Ballistic Missile Defence Organization

ADVANCED TECNLOGY PROGRAM

- 4 annual competitions, to-date
- Total funds committed - $515 million ($247 - government, $268 - private)
- Range of awards: $500,000 → $20M
- 89 awards (23 joint ventures, 66 single applicants)

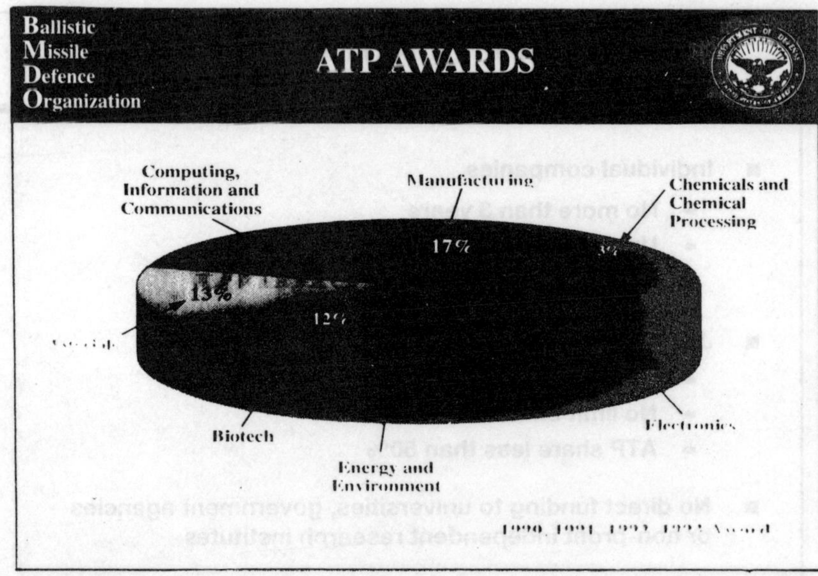
Ballistic
Missile
Defence
Organization
ATP AWARDS
Computing,
Information and
Communications
Manufacturing
Chemicals and
Chemical
Processing
17%
13%
12%
Biotech
Energy and
Environment
Electronics

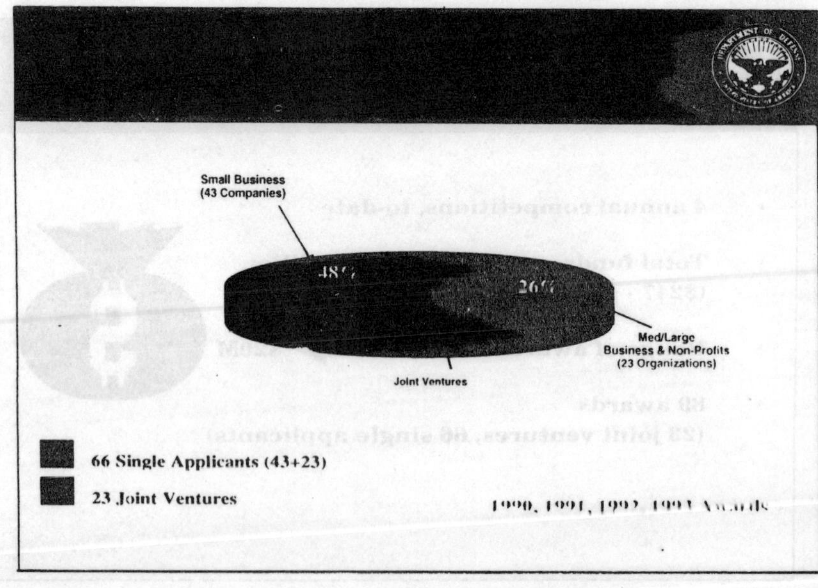
Small Business
(43 Companies)
48%
26%
Med/Large
Business & Non-Profits
(23 Organizations)
Joint Ventures
66 Single Applicants (43+23)
23 Joint Ventures
1990, 1991, 1992, 1993 Awards

ADVANCED TECHNOLOGY PROGRAM

- The President's technology plan expands funding for the ATP to $750M by 1997
- Initial ATP is a solid base to build on:
  - Competitive process
  - No political set-asides
  - Strong market orientation
- Now implementing a process to achieve greatest impact in scaling up ATP

BOTTOM LINE

- ATP will be successful only if industry brings good ideas to the table

THE MANUFACTURING EXTENSION PARTNERSHIP

OBJECTIVE OF MEP

HELP SMALLER MANUFACTURERS BECOME MORE COMPETITIVE

- **Implement appropriate advanced technology - core**
- **Use best manufacturing practices - core**
- **Adopt modern business and workforce approaches - essential related services**

. . . all these involve fundamental change in the companies

SMALLER MANUFACTURERS ARE IMPORTANT

- There are 370,000 manufacturing firms with under 500 employees
- Smaller firms make up 98% of all manufacturing establishments
- Smaller firms contribute more than half the value added in manufacturing in the U.S.
- Smaller firms account for 75% of new jobs in manufacturing
- Smaller firms employ 65% of all manufacturing employees (over 8 million jobs)

. . . and

- Smaller firms supply many of the component parts needed by large firms

COMPONENTS OF MEP

- *Manufacturing Technology Centers (MTCs)* - grow to 30, each serving a large population of companies, regionally or sectorally defined
- *Manufacturing Outreach Centers (MOCs)* - grow to 70, each serving a lower concentration
- *State Technology Extension Program (STEP)* - funding and technical support for planning by states, as well as continuing service delivery in sparse areas
- *Links* - the national structure of communications, data systems, evaluation, field agent training, tool development, and linkages with technology sources

WHAT EXTENSION CENTERS DO
(Examples)

- **CORE**
  - Assessment of company needs
  - Undertake fundamental company reshaping
  - Software demonstration/selection
  - Hardware demonstration/selection
  - Field agents working hands-on
  - Technology projects
  - Shared manufacturing/teaching factories
  - Extensive performance measurement
- **ESSENTIAL RELATED SERVICES**
  - Workforce training and workplace organization
  - Business system development
  - Marketing
  - Financing

BARRIERS FACED BY SMALLER MANUFACTURERS

- Lack of awareness of changing technology, production techniques, and business management practices
- Difficulty for owners and managers of small companies to find high-quality unbiased information, advice, and assistance
- Isolation of smaller manufacturers, which have too few opportunities for interaction with other companies in similar situations
- Regulatory environment which creates a disproportionate burden for smaller firms
- Difficulty obtaining operating capital and investment funds for modernization

From *Learning to Change: Opportunities to Improve the Performance of Smaller Manufacturers*, National Academy Press, 1993.

OPERATING PHILOSOPHY

- There are Federal, state, local, private resources and programs in place which relate to the mission
- Establish linkages with existing resources and programs
- Don't duplicate existing resources
- Work with existing programs

TECHNOLOGY REINVESTMENT PROJECT

Technology Development
Issues
• Increased Federal financial support for civilian R&D •Expand Advanced Technology Program •Increase support for manufacturing •Eliminate low priority programs •Ensure more private sector input •More Federal R&D partnerships with industry •Indirect support through tax incentives •Make the R&E tax credit permanent •Change to R&E tax credit •Strengthen the capital gains tax differential •Revise rules for allocating R&D expenditures

TECHNOLOGY REINVESTMENT PROJECT

Technology Diffusion, Commercialization & Use
Issues
• **Technology Transfer** •**Orient Federal labs more to industry needs** •**Ensure more synergy between military and civilian technology and dual use** •**Emphasize technology transfer more** •**Ensure more private sector input** •**Ensure more state input** •**Streamline CRADA process** •**Create stronger tax and capital formation incentives generally** •**Restore the investment tax credit** •**Provide more accelerated depreciation** •**Reform the alternative minimum tax** •**Business assistance** •**Support industrial extension programs** •**Benchmark against foreign competitors** •**Elevate manufacturing as national policy element** •**Reform government procurement**

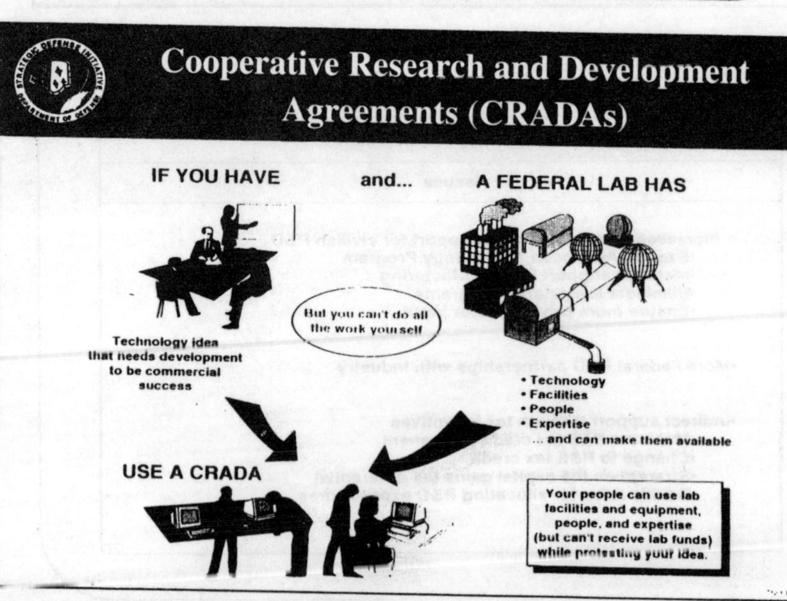

- 1980 Stevenson - Wydler Technology Innovation Act
- 1982 Small Business Innovation Development Act
- 1986 Federal Technology Transfer Act
- 1987 National Defense Authorization Act (DoD Direction)
- 1987 Presidential Executive Order 12591
- 1988 Technology Competitiveness Act

TECHNOLOGY REINVESTMENT PROJECT

Technology Infrastructure
Issues
• Reform education • Workforce upgrading •Strengthen incentives for worker training/education •Expand training •Establish worker training standards •Support school-to-work transition programs •Strengthen dislocated worker assistance • Enhance NII-related infrastructure • Strengthen intellectual property protection • Strengthen U.S. system for gaining acceptance of U.S. standards internationally • Stimulate savings and investment • Integrate all policies affecting technology competitiveness • Strengthen institutional framework for S&T policy • Reform product liability law • Regulatory reform •Interpret regulations more reasonably •Ease antitrust restrictions •Undertake competitiveness impact statements

THE FEDERAL ROLE IN TECHNOLOGY

- How is the government investing in science and technology?
  - Total U.S. R&D > $150B/year
  - Federal government provides:
    - 45% of the funds for U.S. R&D
    - 60% for defense, mostly weapons systems development
    - 15% for health
    - 0.5% for industrial development
- What has changed?
  - Global competition has accelerated the rate of innovation and challenged U.S. industry
  - Post Cold War -> opportunity to redefine our technology investment strategy

THE FEDERAL ROLE IN TECHNOLOGY

- How is the government responding to change?
  - Invest in civilian technology
  - Drive defense toward a dual-use technology base
  - Transfer technology from government labs
  - Continue commitment to basic science

10

Conversion Technologies of the National Academy of Sciences of Ukraine

Anatolij Shpak and Sergei Borovik

The establishments and institutions of the National Academy of Sciences of Ukraine like any highly qualified teams in the world have taken an active part in creating elements, technology, new kinds of military equipment and armament. Accordingly, there was successful and mutually beneficial cooperation among institutes dealing with problems of natural sciences and a number of defense enterprises. During this time scientific teams with highly qualified employees have been organized in order to solve scientific and technological problems of defense strengthening. Special fundamental research undertaken has made significant contribution to general development of fundamental science and scientific and technological advance in industry.

However, the present-day situation has caused dramatic reduction in orders for military purposes. That is why the future and the very existence of many highly professional teams is becoming an acute problem.

Fortunately, our Academy as opposed to other Academies of former Soviet republics, including the Russian Academy, has always been characterized as the one paying special attention to practical application. Fundamental result was just the first step, followed by particular samples of mechanisms, machines, technologies.

Therefore a number of scientific research elaborations carried out according to the orders of military enterprises could be used immediately or after certain improvements in national economy in creating new machines and mechanisms, equipment, as well as consumer goods and modernization of existing technologies.

I believe it would be appropriate to give several examples. Priority conversion directions of National Academy of Sciences of Ukraine include research in materials science, application of new composite, ceramic, thermostable materials in aircraft-, auto-, and ship-building industry.

First and foremost, we mean the following welding technologies:

- welded constructions transformed with transformation coefficient of 50, for space engineering;
- oil storage tanks, dry substances storage, pontoon bridges;
- welding of precise machine-building and radioelectronic products;
- underwater welding and cutting of metals;
- welding and cutting of refractory metals, tungsten, molybdenum, zirkon, niobium.

Then, the following almost completed research is worth mentioning:

- individual means of protection against fire-arms and cold steel weapons;
- materials for laser technology and communications. Ceramic mirrors (cooled and non-cooled) for powerful infrared lasers and space communications;
- soldering of metal-nonmetal units for space engineering;
- fire-proof construction ceramics;
- high-temperature superconducting coatings.

Attention should be paid to domain-acoustic processor, the device employing the effect of memorizing of high-frequency signal by micro magnetic structure of polycrystal medium. It is designated for long-term memorizing (for hours, days) of phase portrait of complex information signal and coordinated filtration of signals with complex structure.

Some years ago the institutes of chemical profile were to solve an important task: working out of processes for transforming liquid rocket fuel – heptile – into practically useful products.

Nowadays our scientists have elaborated the processes of transforming heptile into such products:

- inhibitors of hydrogen sulfide corrosion;
- biologically active compounds for pre-sowing seed treatment during vegetation period (futicides and regulators of plant growth);
- surface-active substances for various purposes, in particular, for detergents;
- accelerators of epoxide resin polymerization;
- medicines;
- polymer materials.

We can give a lot of similar examples. They clearly demonstrate both great potential of our Academy and plenty of unclaimed scientific research and technologies created, specifically, for military industry.

From this follows our point of view concerning conversion problems of scientific teams that predominantly deal with matters of defense. Taking care of preserving scientific schools, actively working research teams with high scientific qualification, it seems logical to change emphasis, i.e. to somewhat reduce new fundamental research (at least, for the time being), and concentrate means and forces on transformation of military high technologies for civil purposes.

This would help retain highly qualified specialists, reduce anxiety regarding their future, and make less painful transition of scientific teams to market-driven economy.

Possible Ways of Cooperation in the Sphere of Conversion

1. Elaboration of methods of early prediction of natural disasters (hurricanes, sandstorms, volcano eruptions, ice hummocks) using space-based side vision radio locators.
2. Creation of general automated database of ionosphere parameters and a system of ecological monitoring of the Earth, specifically, earthquake prediction by using non-coherent scattering observatories.
3. Organization of joint venture concerning production of millimeter-range wavelength medical equipment for curing digestion organs.
4. Working out of data processing multiprocessor systems using databases with microwave technology for data exchange.
5. Creation of joint ventures association on developing modern sensor devices
6. Organization of joint venture on elaboration of methods of transforming rocket fuels and explosives into raw material for chemical industry.

11

Military Conversion and Science in the Czech Republic

Stanislav Stach

1. Introduction

The end of the Cold War and of the East-West confrontation, followed by the fall of communism, the break-up of the Warsaw Pact, the rise of new social order in the Central and East Europe, by unification of Germany and withdrawal of Soviet troops from the Czech and Slovak Republic, Hungary, Poland, former GDR and Baltic states, together with a long-term influence of the Confidence and security building measures and signing of Strategic offensive arms and Conventional armed forces in Europe limitation treaties, created an entirely new situation in Europe. The present huge armies and expanded weapon industries, built during the 40 years of the arms race, have lost their purpose and become an encumbrance to the newly formed states, building democracy and market economy. The global political context has always played a decisive role both in development and in reduction of the military production.

Particularly in countries to the East of the Iron Curtain the weapon industry was an example of centrally planned and controlled, state sponsored economy.

Though the processes of restructuralism are taking place parallely in the East and in the West, the revolutionary changes in the former Warsaw Pact countries have reflected themselves in the sphere of weapon industry in an unprecedented way. The key word for the whole period of the four last years became the term "conversion". The conversion of weapon industry, in spite of its particular character, has become an important phenomenon of the overall transformation of the society.

From the wider point of view we can include under this term:

- the limitation of the military budget and transfer of saved means to other peaceful ends,
- the release of military personnel, its requalification and inclusion into the civil sphere,
- the civil utilization of abandoned military installations,
- the peaceful application of some military equipment,
- the military industry suppressing and its transformation to peaceful programs,
- the military research and development installation's transformation to peaceful programs,
- the economic, social, environmental and other consequences of the withdrawal of foreign forces,
- the regional problems, including questions of the infrastructure, services, unemployment, stemming from the military industry conversion, armed forces down-sizing and relocation, and the foreign troops withdrawal.

The Czech republic's military industry is being influenced by many circumstances simultaneously, and it is not easy to decide which of them is the most influential. To the main factors, whose consequence is the limitation of the weapons production and the military industries conversion we can count:

- The Czech armed forces and its equipment down-sizing,
- The Czech Republic's military budget reduction,
- The Warsaw Pact and Eastern markets of the COMECON member states disintegration,
- The rise of insolvency in many of East European and Asian states,
- The political decision of the Czech government not to support the weapons production and to end this production in the quickest way, not regarding the price paid, from humanitarian reasons,

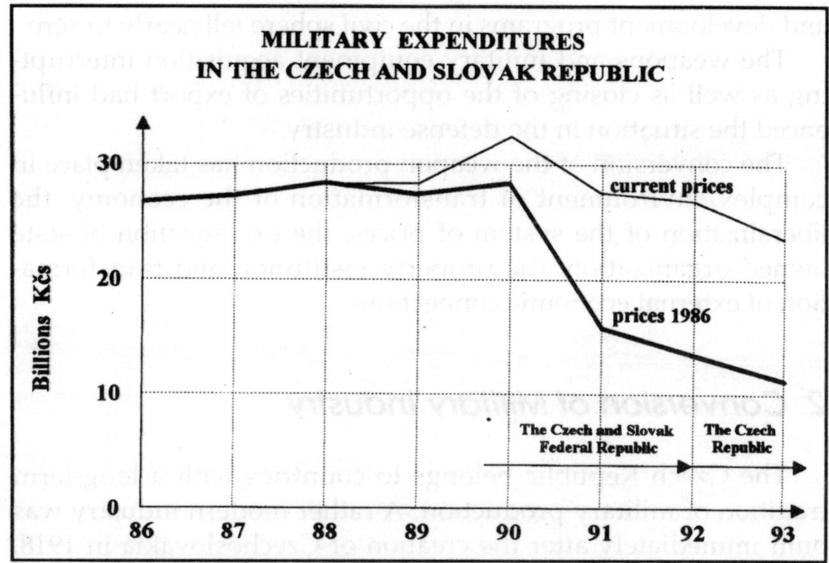

Fig. 1 - Military expenditures in the Czech and Slovak republic

- The necessity of a gradual improving of interoperability and compatibility of the Czech Armed Forces with the NATO countries.

The Czech Armed Forces was reduced from approximately 200,000 men of the former Czech and Slovak Federal Republic in 1989 to 65,000 men of the present Czech Armed Forces at the end of the 1994, that is to about 32%, or to 42% regarding the division of the Czech and Slovak Republic in 1992/93. The real military budget was reduced from 28 billions Kcs in 1989 to about 11 billion Kcs in 1994 (in 1986 process) that is to 39% respectively to 59% as is seen from Fig. 1.

As a result of this trend the acquisition of any weapons and military equipment was stopped, purchases of spare parts were severely reduced, and financial resources allocated to research and development programs in the civil sphere fell nearly to zero.

The weapons and military equipment acquisition interrupting as well as closing of the opportunities of export had influenced the situation in the defense industry.

The conversion of the weapon production has taken place in complex environment of transformation of the economy, the liberalization of the system of prices, the privatization of state owned organization, the property restitution and transformation of external economic connections.

2. Conversion of Military Industry

The Czech Republic belongs to countries with a long-term tradition of military production. A rather modern industry was built immediately after the creation of Czechoslovakia in 1918, on the basis of companies Skoda Plzen, Scheillier and Bellot Praha, Zbrojovka Brno, CKD Praha, CZ Strakonice, Explosia Semtin and others. Especially Skoda Plzen company has undergone the important development in this period. It owned, before the Second World War, the ship building company in Komarno, weapon factory in Brno, aircraft companies AVIA in Prague and Kunovice, car factory Laurin and Klement in Mladá Boleslav, machine and bridge works in Adamov, ammunition and gun factory in Dubnice n. Váhom and an export organization Omnipol. Most of these companies belong still to the basis of the Czech industry.

The Czechoslovak industry was one of the ten most important exporters of weapons in the between-the-wars period, and in 1934 and 1935 held the first place among them. The main items of the military export were infantry and artillery weapons, explosives, and later on special military vehicles, including tanks. Also the aviation industry developed well. Most of the companies, concentrated into robust syndicates, were private owned.

During the Second World War the Czech industry served to the fascist Germany. Many installation were further rebuilt and extended.

After the Second World War, the communists' victory, and beginning of the East-West confrontation the weapon industry started to grow again and concentrated on licensed production of Soviet equipment. The center of gravity of military production began to move to Slovakia. New factories were built e.g.: ZTS Martin, ZVL Povázská Bystrica, ZVT Banská Bystrica, ZVS Dubnica n. Váhom, Vihorlat Snina, Tesla Liptovsky Hrádock, Mostárna Brezno, VSS Košice, PS Povázská Bystrica, ZVS Meopta Bratislava and other. Production delimitation was accompanied by transfer of expert to Slovakia.

The professional level of the aircraft industry grew substantially in after-the-war period, especially in the Czech Republic. The licensed production of Soviet Mig jet planes brought a technological breakthrough, and enable later an independent development and production of airplanes. The L29, L39 and L59 types of aircraft production represented 66% of the world production of training airplanes, up to 1966. New factory for aircraft engines was built in Slovakia in Povázská Bystrica.

The core of the military industry specialized on production of tanks and armored personnel carriers, was created in 1956-1962, and allowed lately for expanded production. The military production culminated in the CSFR in 1987-1988, when more then 100 factories, about 73,000 of workers directly and about 50-60,000 indirectly participated in weapons production. About 70% of the production was exported. The military factories were concentrated in the Váh region in Slovakia, in South Moravia and the Prague region in the Czech Republic.

The period of rapid decline of the military production in the Czech and Slovak Republic began after the 1989 revolutionary changes (see Fig. 2). The 1992 production comprises about 20% of the 1988 production of weapons.

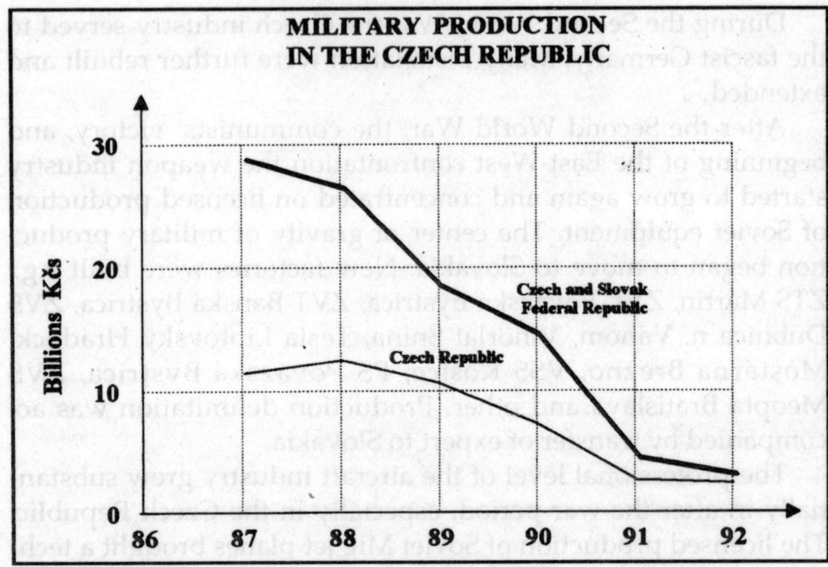

Fig. 2 - Military production in the Czech Republic

The severe restriction of opportunities to sell the military products both abroad and at home caused the necessity to seek ways how to transform the military factories to produce civil products. Such transformation was complicated by recession in other spheres of the internal economy, that showed no interest for new machine products.

The government, under the pressure of producers, decided to help financially during the first stages of the process of conversion, and released some fiscal means for this purpose. About 1.5 billion Kcs in 1991 (0.3 billion for the Czech Republic) and about 1 billion Kcs in 1992 (0.2 billion for the Czech Republic) was used for this purpose. Gradually about 100 conversion programs were prepared, from which only part was realized. However, the producers were bound mostly to resolve the situation without much help, or simply stop the production.

The split of the Czech and Slovak Republic into two independent sovereign states, at the end of 1992, made the process of conversion in the Czech Republic more easy. The majority of non easily convertible factories, producing tanks and armored vehicles, was concentrated in Slovakia. Only the more easily convertible industries were left in the Czech Republic: aircraft and electronic factories, production of hand-held weapons, precision engineering and optics factories, production of equipment for protection against the chemical, bacteriological and nuclear weapons etc. In addition these factories were often technically equipped, staffed by qualified personnel, with good working discipline, and used to quality control requirements.

3. Conversion in the Field of Science, Research and Development

The military complex of the Czech and Slovak Federal Republic consisted, of course, also of the research and development facilities associated usually to production factories, or ministerial research institutions. Some of these institutions functioned within the framework of the armed forces. Some institutes of national academies of science and at the universities and colleges participated on long-term scientific programs, financed by the Ministry of Defense. Comparatively modern research and testing institutes were built within the military forces.

The armed forces supported scientific programs in civil institutions oriented particularly to the sphere of medical and veterinary sciences, chemistry, and protection against toxic and biological weapons, development of advanced materials and technologies, laser technology, infrared technology, millimeter electromagnetic waves, computer, communication and radar technology and new principles of navigation.

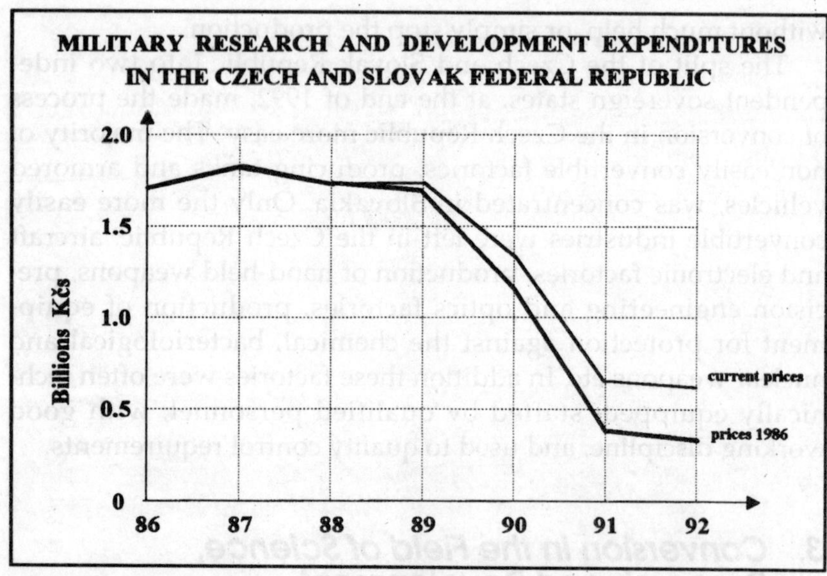

Fig. 3 - Military research and development expenditures in the Czech and Slovak Federal Republic

Some programs in the field of armor, engineering, automobile technology, artillery, rocket technology, training and transport aircraft, reconnaissance and communication, fire control system, ammunition and explosive were in development stage. Some workplaces were specialized on adjustment of the licensed procedures to domestic conditions.

Basically, it should be mentioned, that the science and research in the Czech Republic were never fully militarized. The top scientists were never interested in working on classified projects, especially due to fear that their opportunities to travel and publish the result of research could be limited.

After the 1990, the armed forces gradually stopped to finance the scientific programs in the civil sphere. The conversion of not too wide scientific teams became a constituent part of a wider trend of restructuralisation of scientific institutions. The fall-down of resources allocated to military research is shown in Fig. 3.

At present, even the state does not single out sufficient means for science and research. The salaries in research institutions are substantially lower then in sphere of private enterprise. The transformation of society prefers a quick pay-off. Scientific and research institutes are reducing substantially the number of employees, some inefficient programs are wound-up, some institutes are dissolved. Though the process of privatization involves the scientific institutions only marginally, majority of them have to earn their own living, at least partially. resources are no longer provided globally, but selectively on specific projects, predominantly in the form of grants. Young, talented workers are often seeking and finding self-assertion in international and private companies, or in the sphere of enterpreneurship. Only smaller part of employees is succeeding in applying for foreign or domestic grants, that help them to maintain their standards of living.

But very small portion of scientific workers is leaving the country. If they are going abroad, it is mostly for a temporary stay, they usually return home. Fig. 4 shows the decline of number of workers in the field of research and development.

Among the positive factors of the present process of transformation we can count:

- closer contact with world science,
- higher requirements applied to scientific workers, accompanied by selection of the best,
- higher opportunity of self-assertion, not limited to the national scale.

There are, of course, some negative consequences:

- reduced financial means provided by the state,
- difficult financing of long-term projects, not bringing an immediate pay-off,

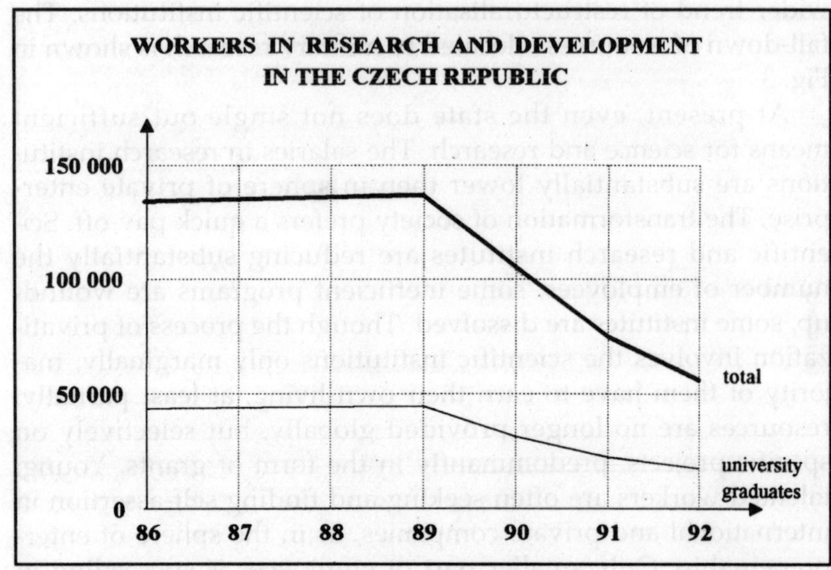

Fig. 4 - Workers in research and development in the Czech republic

- outflow of young and talented workers into the private economy, which offers higher gains.

Especially, the exploratory research is most endangered, and as a result of scarce resources available, is stagnating. Short-term projects, linked to industrial and business needs, bringing immediate profit, are preferred.

4. Conversion and the Sphere of Education

Civil universities and colleges only exceptionally participated on military projects. Officers, and even civil employees in the field of defense were educated mostly in military schools. The conversion of weapons industry concerns the civil schools

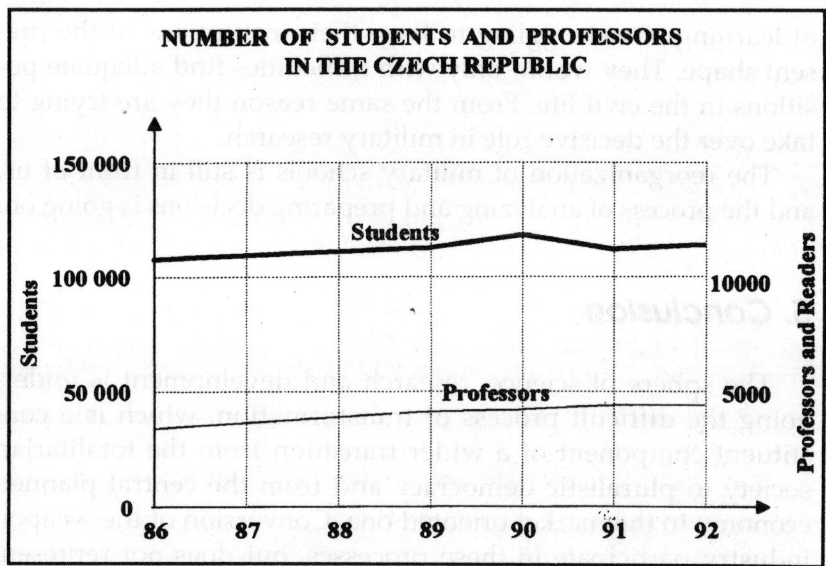

Fig. 5 - Number of students and professors in the Czech Republic

and universities only marginally. The number of students has a steady, slightly increasing trend, uninterrupted by revolutionary changes of the last period (see Fig. 5)

The number of applicants, particularly in liberal arts, exceeds many times the number of vacant places available. It could be expected that the reorganization of the educational system will bring some changes, but only in coming period. It will probably result in higher financial burden put on students and their parents.

A different situation exists in the military educational system. The military schools are still too overstaffed, and the down-sizing and reorganization of the armed forces did not still influenced them. The older, highly qualified employees of military schools, and people specialized in purely military branches of learning, are struggling to keep their institutions in the present shape. They would only with difficulties find adequate positions in the civil life. From the same reason they are trying to take over the decisive role in military research.

The reorganization of military schools is still in front of us, and the process of analyzing and preparing decisions is going on.

5. Conclusion

The sphere of science, research and development is undergoing the difficult process of transformation, which is a constituent component of a wider transition from the totalitarian society to pluralistic democracy and from the central planned economy to the market oriented one. Conversion of the weapon industry participate in these processes, but does not represent the most important part. The science in the Czech Republic was never fully militarized and due to division of the Czech and Slovak Federal Republic into two independent states the most difficult problems of conversion of the heavy weapon industry passed to Slovakia. The center of gravity of the weapon industry in the Czech Republic is the sphere of the aircraft industry, electronics, hand-held weapons, precision engineering and optics, production of ammunition and explosives. The duality of the military and civil production was always presented in these branches, and it is why the factories and linked research and development institutions are comparatively successful in reducing the military production and in transition to the civil one. In addition some new opportunities are outlining themselves in context of inevitable implementation of measures to improve the compatibility and interoperability of weapons and system with NATO member states. This building of compatibility is connected with modernization of equipment and with new request for research.

The transformation of society brings many positive factors, connected with an opening to the world, the exchange of information, and higher mobility of scientific workers.

Concurrently the reduction of resources allocated by the state to science development and to the armed forces brings many organizational, economic, and social problems. The number of workers in research and development is falling. There is connection to higher qualification requirements, and to higher attractivity of jobs in the private sector, especially for younger and talented people. The preference of quick pay-offs and short-time programs brings stagnation into the exploratory research. New pieces of legislation are being elaborated.

The civil educational system is comparatively stable, system of military schools is waiting for a principal reform.

Any small nation, like the Czech Republic, has to make every effort to utilize all national resources in an optimal way. Even the integrated national resources are not sufficient for an effective development of science. A cooperation with the world scientific community is essential. The expected inclusion of the Czech Republic into the European economic, political and security structures, together with a wider share on common development programs, would play an important role in consolidating the sphere of science and research.

Making use of the top level science and technology is a prerequisite of success in an economic competition. The independent, own scientific base makes possible the transfer of the scientific knowledge, and enables, at the same time, to contribute to solving the global and regional problems.

The armed forces should retain its position as an organization supporting the science progress and to continue in singling out resources for scientific programs out of its budget. Military scientific and research institutions should have to try to build links with analogous institutions abroad. The participation in common projects should be discussed, within the framework of

Partnership for Peace program, with NATO authorities, and, within the framework of the associated partnership, with the WEU institutions. The military schools should try to be included into the network of NATO educational institutions.

Precondition of any cooperation is the knowledge of languages. Especially in the field of military the language barrier is more important than unified weapons.

At the same time, maintaining and edifying the cultural level of the nation means to allow as many young people as possible to get as wide education as possible, in spite of the risk that they will not work exactly in the same field of activity they studied. Including the wide opportunity to study in schools abroad.

SOCIO-ECONOMIC CONSIDERATIONS OF MILITARY CONVERSION'S IMPACTS ON SCIENCE AND TECHNOLOGY

12

Social Conditions for Science: Are there too many Scientists and Engineers?

Horácio Menano

The political and socio-economic changes produced in eastern and central European countries in the last five years have had enormous consequences in local conditions for Science. This was firstly the immediate result of the decrease in funding for research and technological activities and could be seen as one of the most important factors in generating the massive brain drain prevalent in these countries **(1,2)**.

Another important consequence of the political changes have been the modifications produced in the industrial-military complexes of the two former blocs. It was to be expected that this would take a form of decreasing research activities either by particular decision-making or from diversion of funds. In either case consequences would follow.

It is necessary to distinguish the consequences of sudden decrease of the activities in state owned institutions engaged in defense research activities and the situation of private research institutions with large defense contracts facing the sudden disappearance of important funds. In both cases the non availability of funds will in the end produce pressures for the dismissal of scientists and engineers. In the first case it seems that the purpose of the institution and even its existence can be put into question if there is no possibility to restructure it through some form of transition toward "civilian" objectives. In the second case the decrease in funds is more easily absorbed and the institution itself is, normally, not in danger. In both cases there is, together with the (brain) loss of scientists and engineers, a change in the internal (social) conditions for work and in many cases institutional deterioration.

From the year 1990 on both these situations were very evident in the former Soviet Union and central European countries but also became more and more prevalent in the other European countries and in the United States and Canada. The situation of conversion of military into civilian **R&D** is becoming very important everywhere.

On the other hand it is now clear that this important and specific surplus of scientists and engineers is developing in an environment where a general change in conditions for Science is felt almost everywhere.

This situation can be described globally as if the market for (new) scientific institutions and for scientists and engineers is not expanding anymore. It can also be described as a situation where there are **already too many scientists and engineers**. Some very dramatic examples show particular aspects of the general situation as can be seen in the case of the decision to terminate the Superconducting Super Collider (S.S.C.) Lab. One year after the decision was taken from around the Lab's 1100 member scientific and technical staff only 100 remain. From the 200 physicists only 72% found new jobs and from those only about half found jobs in their own original field. Others found jobs in computer, electronics and even in financial industries **(3)**.

The question can be now asked: is this an extreme example specially related to the field of high energy and theoretical physics and also only seen in this very short term?

It seems on the contrary that the problems are very broad as many papers published in very recent months show.

Following the test case of the S.S.C. collapse let us look at some of the discussions now being held in the USA not only because they are very openly being described in a rather well documented way but because, regarding our main theme on conversion and world-wide brain-drain, this country has always been one of the preferred places of attraction for scientists and also an inexhaustible reservoir.

Interestingly enough the series of papers on **"Science Careers: Playing to Win"** published on the **Science** issue of September 23 last **(4)** starts with the statement from David Goldstein of the California Institute of Technology saying **"The expansionary era of American Science has come to an end"**.

As we described above the situation is related with the end of Cold War and in the last few years with recession induced corporate and government funding cuts. The figures of unemployment for scientists as a class were still rather low, in 91 around 1.4%, but in certain areas the figures were unprecedently high as was the case for recipients of new mathematics PhD, with an unemployment rate of 8.9%. This situation seems to have a tendency to be worsening in the last years. Certain fields are suffering less than others as is the case for biology. Nevertheless these descriptions tell very little as they do not reflect the very important dislocations of science posts inside the scientific institutions and industry with young scientist holding patterns of repeated **"postdocs"** and the rise of researchers holding temporary posts.

It is now not only a big challenge for the individual scientist to start or maintain himself in a scientific career in academe or in industry but also a great challenge for institutions themselves to adapt and change. As examples there have been meetings on "reinventing the research university" and on changing for a new-paradigm graduate student and also recommendations to the United States government to undergo a shift in the way it supports research, moving from a system dominated by grants for investigator-initiated proposals to one preferring contracts for targeted research. As could be expected there is no unanimity on these views. The need to further analyse the state of the Science and Technology system in the United States has now been translated into a very broad study to be conducted by a panel of distinguished scientists coordinated by the chairmanship of Frank Press former president of the National Academy of Sciences and to be finalised in December 1995. The report is to be seen as one to have objectives comparable to the report by Vannevar Bush titled "Science: The Endless Frontier" which laid the foundations for the growth of research in the United States after the Second World War. The report was requested by United States Senate and will deal with the setting of new **R&D** priorities and it will supplement the very recent White House report on basic science **"Science in the National Interest"**.

When we now turn our attention to the general situation for Science in the European countries we will find, in spite of the enormous differences in institutional structures and constrictions related to specific national systems, many of the problems referred to above. Some of the difficulties can be seen in the very fierce discussions regarding the restructuring and funding of research centers that are now being pursued in Germany, Britain and France and probably in all the others. In all places there is, with the acceptance of a system of contracts for targeted research a clear demand for an increase or at least a maintenance of core funding from government sources. Simultaneously it is apparent that the great proportion, in European terms, of temporary posts for scientists and engineers are now producing concern for the build up of acceptable careers for individual scientists or scientists to be. Two interesting examples referring to science education come from Britain where there is a very great decrease in the number of candidates to science degrees in the British universities **(5)** and this has started a movement toward the reform of the A level system, the **"gold standard"** for admission. Another reform would be a change in the British PhD system introducing a first year for a new **"Master of Research"** qualification that could also be used for direct employment in industry.

All those signs and symptoms to use a typical medical

nomenclature, are sufficient to indicate the existence of not only a discomfort in the global scientific community but of a malady. This malady has been certainly aggravated by the acute political changes, local economic disturbances and rather general recession, but must have originated in a model that behaves as if there is no need for an increase in the number of scientists pursuing a career with some degree of stability.

I personally do not believe this is the case and that there is a great need to address ourselves to what is necessary to maintain progress in Science and what are its necessary social conditions **(6)**.

REFERENCES

1. ANGELL, I. O. AND KOUZMINOV, V. A., 1990 Report of the Working Party on Brain Drain Issues in Europe. Tech. Rep. nr. 3 UNESCO-ROSTE.
2. BIGGIN, S. AND KOUZMINOV, V. A., 1993, Proceedings of the International Seminar on "Brain Drain Issues in Europe". Tech. Rep. nr. 15, UNESCO-ROSTE.
3. ROUSH, W., Colliding Forces, Life After the S.C.C., Science 266: 532, 1994.
4. HOLDEN, C., Science Careers, Science 26: 1905, 1994.
5. The Economist. Science Education. August 27th, 1994.
6. GANELIUS, T., 1983, Progress in Science and its Social Conditions. Proceedings of a Nobel Symposium, Pergamon Press.

13
Problems of Military Conversion and Science in Russia

Nicolay Malyshev

The public cataclysms in Russia did not pass the sphere of science. First of all the slump of its national and state authority, a sharp reduction of its financing give evidence for it. The expenses for science have come down from 5.1 % in 1990 to 3.1 of national income in 1993.

Did science find itself by chance in such a position?

The development of science was determined mainly by the political guidelines of the state. Science in the USSR was not always an ingenuous productive force, but till recent years it was a factor of national pride. In this sphere it was taken as a matter of course not to calculate the expenses and losses during the implementation of state objectives, such as the creation of the powerful research and experimental base in the sphere of nuclear physics, development of inter-continental ballistic missiles, the opening up of outer space.

The fall of financing in 1990 has shown that the state was not already able to play a role of a generous patron. The danger of destruction of many famous scientific schools, research teams, important scientific directions which represented both national and world pride had become the reality.

By this time the supply of science with the material and technical resources sharply worsened which was already insufficient. In this sphere we were always becoming detached from the industrial developed countries, and whereas science in the West had been technically re-arming, our lag was turned into difficult overcoming alienation. By the end of 1980 the main funds of science had put together less than 2% of the main funds of our economy. One of the main component of the general crisis in Russia is a disparity of the level of material, technical and information base to the objectives of the modern science.

Science in Russia which had taken the path of reform, was from the first steps excluded out of the sphere of great attention from the side of high level leaders, authorities of all levels.

In 1991 the average strength of the scholars and employees was reduced to 55 thousand men or by 1.8%; in 1992 - to 768 thousand men or by 25% and in 1993 - to 407 thousand men or by 17.6%. The scientific sector of military branches (more than 700 research institutes and labs) had lost about 18% of its strength together with the significant reduction of important R&D. As a whole during that period of time the strength of scholars and employees was reduced by 1230 thousand men or by 39.3%. According to the evaluations, in 1994 the strength of employed people in this sphere will be reduced by 10-12% and in 1995 - still by 7-8%. The significant reduction of personnel had taken place during the past period in the branch sector of science.

The collapse of the USSR had brough heavy consequences which were connected with the rupture of not only economic but also scientific relations. In the sphere of galvanics, for instance, Russia was left with science but without appropriate manufacturers (they are now in Ukraine and Lithuania). In the sphere of welding, on the other hand, Russia had lost the main scientific centre of the former USSR - Paton's Institute, but Russia has a part of manufacture. And such examples could be continued. In the R&D sphere Russia had lost a part of its property including experimental bases and installations which were left out of Russia. Such situation has been seen also in the military sector of Russian economy.

Because of consumption reduction in renewal and increase in production quality, level of technology and equipment, the production demand for scientific and technical production was reduced. In 1993 1382 new kinds of goods were produced in comparison with 2404 in 1990 what is less by 42.5 %. Specific gravity of new goods in the total value of production came down in 1993 to 3.4% in comparison with 6.5% in 1990, including absolutely new goods - 1.6% against 3%.

The value of direct treaties of industrial plants with the scientific bodies was sharply cut. The value of searching R&D in the sphere of creation of necessary scientific and technical surplus in common value of research works of scientific institutes and labs of machinery building was cut from 26% in 1991 till 0.8 in 1993. The quantity of completed R&D and produced models of new technique in machinery building was reduced 11 times during the last 3 years.

The situation in military and political sphere had been also changed: the interest of authorities to the military sector, including its base of basis - military branch of science feeding many branches of knowledge, had become lower (Fig.1), see tables 1 and 2.

At present more than 45% of organizations network which implement the scientific R&D, are situated in the territory of some regions. They are: Moscow and Moscow region, S.-Petersburg and Leningrad, Novosibirsk, Sverdlovsk, Rostow and Nijnegorodskaya regions and some other republics.

Unfortunately, till nowadays Russia had no a regional scientific policy. Now the main principle of such policy is to avoid extremities: to shift off the responsibility of its realization onto the Centre or the local authorities that in both cases would lead to undesirable consequences in the development both of science and of regions.

For averting such irreversible processes taking place in scientific and technical sphere, the measures on reorientation of the state scientific and technical policy are performed.

The special bodies were organized by the decree of the President of the Russian Federation. They are: Russian Fund of fundamental research for support of originating scientific projects, which are mainly performed by the institutes of Russian Academy of Science (it receives 3% of budget of civilian R&D), Russian nonbudget Fund of technological development for financing R&D and measures on production of new kinds of goods.

The Government of the Russian Federation had adopted a decision about creation of a Fund of stimulation of the development of small forms of scientific and technical sphere. It has been investing into this fund 0.5 % of allocations from federal budget for science development.

The analysis of effectiveness and utilization in 1992-1993 of federal budget means for civilian R&D in military sector shows that the distribution of means through the great quantity of organizations and manufacture's has taken place instead of the concentration of these means for the conservation and development of high scientific and technical potential of Russian science in the interest of national economy and using of it in the key scientific and technical directions which secure and consolidate the world level of home elaborations.

In 1992-1993 in the Ministry of Science of Russia a huge work on organization of State scientific centres of Russian Federation was performed with the aim of conservation of leading scientific schools of world level, development of country's scientific potential in the sphere of fundamental, searching and applied investigations and also training of high qualified scientific personnel.

It should be noted that in 1994-1995 preferential development will be given to that R&D which is implemented according to the programmes of the state scientific centres. Creation of such centres will lay essentially the foundation of strategic line of concrete support of the leaders of Russian science. The created centres can already now take under its tutelage the main branches of national economy, realize the elaborations not only non-yielding to international level, but in some directions overcoming it. In the framework of the programmes of such centres there is anticipated the development of investigations and elaborations in the sphere of aircraft and space technique, power engineering (including nuclear one), new materials, electrical engineering, electronics, optics, optoelectronics, laser technique, genetics, biology, microbiology and some other forward-looking directions.

At present according to the Decree of the President of the Russian Federation N 939 from June 22, 1993 and the resolution of the Government of the Russian Federation N 1346 from December 25, 1993 the status of state scientific centre was awarded to 48 scientific organizations more than half of which are related to the military sector. The interdepartmental commission on scientific and technical policy had recommended to award such status also to 8 scientific bodies. Thus, the total number of state scientific centres will reach 70-75.

The main priority will be given as usual to the fundamental scientific elaborations which are a source of new knowledge, a base for the development of applied R&D.

It is envisaged to concentrate the work of the branch academies on the priority directions.

To change fundamentally the situation we need to reach an activization of participation of Russian science and particularly its military sector in international technical co-operation, an access of Russian high technologies to the world market, to draw foreign investments for support of Russian science and participation in taking decisions in the sphere of science, engineering and economy.

All these measures need creation of an absolutely new system of legislation for ensuring the scientific and technical activity.

14

Culture of Peace and Transformation of Science

Boris Borisov

"Since wars begin in the minds of men,
it is in the minds of men
that the defenses of peace must be constructed"

These are the first words of UNESCO's Constitution, written and adopted almost fifty years ago, just after the Second World War was over.

Ever since, the United Nations Educational, Cultural and Scientific Organization as the whole UN system has witnessed drastic and sometimes dramatic developments in world history.

Today, a unique convergence of historical facts has put the abolition of war on the agenda. This certainly does not mean an end to the violence of war, it means rooting out the culture of war that has come to dominate our institutions and therefore our everyday lives.

Today, more than ever it is necessary to seek positive ways to resolve conflicts by working out our behavior and attitudes.

Today with the end of the Cold War and the dissolution of the superpower blocks it is necessary to involve everybody in the peace building process.

Today new peace-building structures are needed to help transition from a culture of war to a culture of peace.

It imposes a re-ordering of global priorities - financial, educational, scientific, cultural, social, human to tackle global problems - from social injustice to the environment that threaten our security and well-being.

In response to the challenge of peace-building, UNESCO,

which has always undertaken long term actions to build the foundations of peace through its fields of competence, is to assume a new and dynamic role, aimed at encouraging and reinforcing a culture of peace.

As Federico Mayor, UNESCO Director General said, "it is time to get history to lay down its arms. To teach our children the history of power, but not of knowledge, the history of war but not of culture... Therefore change we must. We must learn to pay the price of peace just as we had to pay the price of war. We shall have to set fresh priorities".

It is therefore no surprise that UNESCO's Culture of Peace Programme puts so much emphasis on the ability of each individual, each community, from the grass roots up, to build and enhance peace. What is even more important is to persuade policy makers and leaders of states to adopt the attitude of culture of peace.

One of the documents that the Executive Board examined at its recent 145th session in October-November 1994 was entitled: "The culture of peace programme: from national programmes to a project of global scope. The very title speaks of the necessity to start from a given country. It supposes that any process becomes the object of national policy only if the state is interested in it.

If this is the case, the state should formulate an objective. A system of measures and activities, planned and implemented, represent the state policy towards this process.

Take the concrete case of Russia, in particular the actual state policy towards science, and more particular towards conversion.

Let us start from positive results. The state has removed all artificial ideological and administrative obstacles which seriously hindered international scientific cooperation.

Undoubtedly science has become more open and democratic.

At the same time in the changing social and economic formation science in Russia has faced dramatic difficulties, which could be overpassed only with a resolute and active support of the state and society in general.

At present the situation with science in Russia remains very alarming.

Some expert in Russia estimated that sums allotted by the State for scientific research have been reduced by some 30 times. The share of state allotments for science in the gross product in Russia has reached an extremely dangerous level - only 0.5 percent.

According to the State Committee for Statistics only 17 percent of scientists have salaries that exceed the officially established minimum, whereas the average salary of scientific worker occupies the 10th place out of eleven leading branches of economy.

A post-graduate grant in the prestigious Moscow Physics Technology Institute in August 1994 was 25 thousand roubles, which means that it is at least 5 times less than minimum. This certainly does not correspond to the qualifications and complicity of work performed. And as a logical result - a large scale internal and external brain drain. To understand this situation it is necessary to go into history.

It is quite obvious that this situation has not occurred all of a sudden.

Fundamental science in Russia was developed in its own way and mainly with the help of its own resources. By the beginning of the twentieth century Russian fundamental science gained recognition in the world.

It is important to note that Russian science in spite of many difficulties and losses (emigration, arrests, ideological cleanings etc.) managed to survive during the post revolutionary period and the time of Stalin dictature.

The rise of Russian science coincides with the period of Khrouschev when its rating was extremely high in the country and in the world. It was prestigious for sons of party leaders to choose scientific careers. The sixties were the period of "lyrics and physicists".

The situation changed during what we call "stagnation period", under Brezhnev's rule, when strategic decision of the development of science were taken by non competent administrators. At this period we witnessed the creation of many secret scientific institutions (so called "boxes") with numerous scientific staff but with very low input. Practically all of them were oriented towards research in one way or another linked with military utilization.

It is sufficient to say that seventy percent of the total budget of the country went to military purposes at that time.

On the other hand there was a policy to cover the whole spectre of sciences to show to the world that we had leading schools in all branches of science. Instead of concentrating on major disciplines there was evident waste of money, scientist's energy and output without visible results.

That was the reason why scientific and technical revolution in the western countries occurred in the late seventies and in the eighties left the Soviet Union scientifically and economically far behind.

At the same time science has become one of the most active social detonators which led the country to the collapse of the communist system and to the democratic revolution of 1991. Let us remember the role of Russian scientists in opposition to the official regime, just to cite Pyotr Kapitsa and Andrei Sakharov.

To sum up, many difficulties we experience now are in many respects connected with military oriented science and with the abandon of so called "defensive conception". Military oriented industry complex which produced fighters, tanks and guns and in which millions of people, including scientists, is facing the crucial problem: how to survive, converting the industry for production of consumption goods and to what extent.

I am personally convinced that a state like Russia with its enormous territory and thousands of kilometers of its borders and its geopolitical role in the world must have military oriented industry, probably several times smaller but several times more effective than the current one. But at the same time we must think of today and of tomorrow - so that converted branches of industry will have modern automation technologices which can be created only with the help of science.

These objectives can be achieved only when they become the object of state policy.

I consider that after a sort of "catastrophism" to use the expression of Russian ambassador to France Academician Ryzhov, a depressive feeling which was characteristic for the years 1991-1993 not only for simple citizen but also for many politicians we are coming now to the understanding of the necessity of psychological stabilization. To achieve stabilization it is absolutely vital to launch a national programme of culture of peace.

I think it is symptomatic that the main theme during the meeting of Mr. Mayor, Director General of UNESCO with President B. Eltsin was culture of peace in the minds of men. As President B. Eltsin stated, Russia is willing to cooperate in the development of the Programme "Culture of peace". Russia is interested in the creation of a national programme, which would include an all embracing system of education of the entire population for peace democracy and human rights. I believe that transformation of science, oriented to the peaceful conversion would constitute an important element of the programme.

It gives to all of us an optimistic view for the future.

As concerns the concrete proposals of cooperation of Russia with UNESCO in the field of sciences I would like to point out the following:

1. As a follow up the Memorandum of cooperation between

Russian Academy of Science and UNESCO, the Russian Federation is disposed to conclude an agreement about realization in Russia of major innovation projects in the field of fundamental sciences. They may present particular interest, for the proposal to make use of unique and costly Russian scientific stands, polygones and equipment, which in the west would cost a fortune. This could be realized by creation of a foundation for support of fundamental sciences under the auspices of UNESCO or with participation of western countries interested in it.

2. We consider it necessary to reinforce our cooperation in the field of protection of environment with due account of the conception of sustainable development adopted by the Rio Conference in 1992.
3. We are interested in cooperation in the field of monitoring and forecasting of earthquakes, especially regarding the measures of preventive character.
4. We would like to be associated with UNESCO initiatives in the field of ecologically safe, new and non traditional sources of energy and in drawing up of the conception of global energy strategy for the coming Solar Summit in 1995.
5. We are ready to share with UNESCO conceptual ideas and practical experience in the field of creation of ecologically clean settlements within the mandate of the Organization.
6. As a matter of particular interest we are looking forward to an integration of Russian universities and higher education institutions in the worldwide system of science and education, in particular by a wider use of UNESCO possibilities to offer short-term grants for young scientists to carry out common scientific research.
7. In view of positive experience of cooperation of Russian scientists and specialists with ROSTE in tackling major problems of military conversion and "brain drain" and carrying international expertise in the field of scientific and techno-

logical policy and defining the basic foundations of legislation on energy resources we consider important for us to continue our cooperation in the legislative and normative fields.

8. We are ready to make efforts to seek for budgetary and especially for extrabudgetary resources to initiate new projects and we hope UNESCO would take necessary actions to further develop cooperation with Russian science.

It goes without saying that these proposals are not exhaustive. To implement them successfully Russia needs political and psychological stabilization and stability, and western states should be fully aware of this necessary and cooperate with Russia correspondingly for mutual benefit.

15
Intellectual Migration and Technological Innovation

João Caraça

1. About Knowledge, Language and People

The point about intellectual migration is to understand what is knowledge and where it resides. Knowledge can no longer be envisaged as a mysterious fluid, flowing in and out of countries and walls, sometimes embedded in machines, sometimes encoded in documents, sometimes even broadcasted electronically.

Knowledge resides in human bodies, like physical strength, and the whole issue is about capacities of human bodies, organized in groups, societies, nations, etc.

Unlike physical strength however, knowledge does not add simply, unfortunately. Take two men of equal physical strength. It is easy to understand that given proper communication between them they can combine their efforts to, say, pull a load of stones twice as heavy as one of them would be able to pull, alone. What about the knowledge of that couple of two men? Is it double of the knowledge of one of them? Clearly no. Suppose they are both unskilled workers speaking the same language. Then it is easy to admit that the total knowledge of the system of two men is equal to the knowledge of each one of them.

Take as a further example a legion of 10 000 soldiers. With proper training and coordination the physical effect of that legion is very close to 10 000 times the power of a single soldier. What about its total military knowledge? Clearly, it is bigger than that of the individual soldier and clearly also it cannot be obtained simply by multiplying by 10 000 the value corresponding to the soldier level. Here, we assume that the purpose of training, coordination, and command is to enable that legion to function collectively (through the use of proper communication channels) with a total knowledge corresponding to the military knowledge of its general.

Therefore knowledge is not additive, unlike material things, such as energy. Further, knowledge resides in each human body (with different levels and values depending on each individual person) and can be represent by the language, or languages, each human being employs. It is tempting to ascribe a first measure of the "quantity of knowledge" to the number of words each individual human being is able to use in its own daily and professional life. In this case, the military knowledge of a general is maybe only 100 times bigger than that of each rank soldier (500 words for a soldier versus 50 000 words or "memory positions" for a general). But it is this immense language advantage that allows him to coordinate (if communication channels, i.e. officers, sergeants, corporals, function adequately) a physical power 10 000 bigger than, supposedly, his own.

We see thus the power of knowledge, language and communication. The role of language is not only that of a <u>medium</u>, enabling the human being to relate to the world around him, including his fellow human beings, but also that of a <u>repository</u>, representing the capacity of forcing and directing his interaction with it, and thus his ability to survive.

The purpose of organizations, of institutions, is to enable through communication the creation of higher, more complex languages, and the "election" to command of the person which generates and manages a higher repository of knowledge.

Several levels of knowledge (and of language) must be considered *.

---

* João Caraça and Manuel M. Carrilho "A new paradigm in the organization of knowledge", Futures 1994 <u>26</u> (7) pp. 781-786.

First, *tacit knowledge,* governing the relationship of the human being with the world as a whole (the outside world and his own group) experienced particularly as the confrontation of two orders, the "objective" and the "subjective". It is the level of the organization of knowledge which corresponds to what can be defined as "common knowledge", the type of knowledge which is not taught explicitly to us, but which we learn by "exposure" in our own society. It is the level of knowledge of the unskilled worker. Clearly this level has evolved with historical times, but not in a simple linear progression.

Second, we have to define a level of *explicit knowledge* in which language emerges as its definite operator, through the creation of "specialized languages" leading to the affirmation of the identity and the diversity of groups inside a community, and corresponding to a growing level of complexity in the interaction between man and his world: that of "intersubjectivity". Explicit knowledge is associated with the regime of specialized information.

Third, emerging from the level of explicit knowledge through a permanent process of increasing complexity in the relationship between man and his world, the density and intensity of communication processes leads intersubjectivity to be replaced by an enlarged "interactivity", which in turn correspond to languages of higher precision. This is the level of *disciplinary knowledge,* the context in which disciplines, i.e. sciences, philosophy, ethics, aesthetics, appear. Disciplines are associated with larger and highly developed repositories of meanings.

It is in this light that we must treat the effect of knowledge and communication in any area. For instance, if we deal with economic activity, we have to understand what are the intellectual levels of the various segments of the population, how the diverse institutions are organized, and which rules of overall coordination and operation of the economic system are being used. High level repositories of knowledge are effective only if proper institutions are created, or are at work, which take full use of their specific meanings, values and perceptions.

2. About Migrations and Technological Innovation

Migrations are massive motions of people from one territory to others. When people migrate they bring along their language, which embeds their repository of meanings, i.e. their knowledge. People migrate in quest of better social and economic conditions of living.

The U.S.A. can be seen as the result of massive inflows of immigrants which already had a level of tacit knowledge of a quite advanced character (developed in the conditions of a highly sophisticated agricultural-commercial European society, experimenting with industrialisation).

In the physical, material conditions of North America, those massive transfers of tacit knowledge strongly enabled explicitation processes which were then captured by burgeoning institutions. When the power of the State was finally installed after the Civil War the conditions for the functioning of a huge national market were then set. And intellectual migration or brain-drain (i.e. migration of highly specialized or disciplinary knowledge) only acquired an economic visibility in its aftermath.

The notion that science and scientists are "national" emerges only by the end of the XIX century * and is further accentuated by the XX century World Wars. And massive migrations of scientists, in terms of the international scientific community, have arisen mainly in connection with political constraints, ranging from institutional repression to physical terror, like the massive

* Charles Halary "Les exilés du savoir", Editions L'Harmattan, Paris 1994.

transfer of German scientists of Jewish origin during the rise of the III Reich.

With the implosion of the Soviet block, concerns about massive brain-drain have again been voiced. But many misconceptions have also been diffused.

In a recent paper by researchers of the Russian Centre for Science Research and Statistics * it is pointed out that the structure of the active population and that of the emigrants is very similar. This means that there is no specific brain-drain factor. Normal motivations (like ethnic ones, for sure) are at work when looking at emigration globally.

But of course one cannot minimize the loss of intellectuals and of scientists in a given country. The institutions they belonged to, if they were employed at the commanding level, will sure be retarded in their operation and severely handicapped if whole sectors are disbanded. A terrible issue is vested in the ability of the emergent new economy, with its new rules of the game, to cope with it.

Not all scientists leave the country though. Many of them simply leave the science and technology system to look for jobs in the fast-growing business sector and in administration. And this must be considered as a beneficial effect of this "supposed brain-drain". The level of languages (i.e. knowledge) and attitudes they bring into the economy and its regulatory institutions will have a very important effect in a quicker regeneration of wealth when conditions will become favourable.

As these reflections are concerned solely with potential effects in the field of technological innovation, no mention to related and crucially important security issues has been made.

But a final point should not be overlooked. The emigration

---

* E.F. Nekipelova, L.M. Gokhber and L.E. Mindeli "Emigration of Scientists: Problems, Real Estimations", Russian Academy of Sciences, Moscow 1994.

of bright and eminent scientists has a devastating effect in the stimulation of intelligent young people for entering scientific careers; thus, the inflow of new and young personnel will probably sharply decrease. This may cause, a generation later, also a decrease in the sophistication of high-level languages and therefore a slow-down in the pace of economic recovery.

16

Considerations on Socio-Economic Consequences of the Restructuring of Military Industry in Italy

Alberto Traballesi

All industrialised countries are experiencing considerable restructuring of the military industrial sector, following public spending cuts. Owing to the fall of the internal market, restructuring was further needed to maintain the competitiveness of this sector on the international market, which is also slackening.

The implication is a loss of jobs, but not necessarily an increase of unemployment, because jobs may increase in other expanding industrial sectors, while being reduced in the military sector.

In a developed country, military industry is only a small share of the entire industrial sector, so in a macroeconomic perspective a reduction of orders deriving from the military sector have almost non existent repercussions in terms of employment on economic development. On the contrary, the effects on technological innovation are more visible, because these are largely technology intensive types of production.

Under the microeconomic and territorial viewpoints, however, it becomes apparent that military factories are unevenly distributed on the national territory, where concentrations are found in specific areas.

Consequently the process of restructuring is extremely important locally and its socio-economic effects have a direct influence on regional economic systems, at least in the short to medium term, particularly in connection with the impact on scientific and technological development, which is certainly also affected by the degree of specialization of individual sectors and by the ensuing competitiveness in the face of sectors other than the military.

The case of Italy does not merely confirm this general picture, it even magnifies it, so a few data on the size of the sector may turn useful.

The Italian military industry accounts for less than 1% of employment in the national industry; it employs 40,000 workers for the production of military equipment and its turnover amounts to 7-8,000 billion Liras. In this context, the internal market absorbs 4,000 billion Liras, including imports, while exports amounted to 1,100 billion Liras in 1993.

The planning of military expenditure over the next few years, being approved by Parliament, and the expected reasonable increase of international market orders, which may occur after regulations on armament transfer is fully adjusted to those of the other European Union countries, indicate that the Italian military industry may rely on a market rapidly approaching an amount of about 6 to 7,000 billion Liras.

In this case, in Italy, the global size of diversification into civilian production would turn out to be limited, as it may involve less than 20% of the labour force of the sector, that is to say from 6 to 8,000 people, as against 6.7 million people employed in the national industry, in which there has been an employment fall by slightly more than 100,000 jobs since 1990.

Territorial distribution of production and related specialization have been left out from the above comments, which outline the presence of a limited balance between supply and demand, in the light of planning made so far.

It is in this connection, however, that the problems of Italian industry are to be found, together with their repercussions on the local socio-economic situation.

Historically the largest part of military industry has developed in northern-western and central-southern well defined areas of the country, where production became highly specialised and armaments were made to meet specific requirements. The identification of their origin and location would require a study of its own and is not relevant here. In particular the aeronautical industry developed in the Turin-Milan-Varese area, the light armament industry developed in the area of Brescia; ship-building is to be found along the Genoa-La Spezia-Leghorn route; ammunitions are produced in the area of Rome, where electronics is also developed; finally the aeronautical industry is also present in the territory of Naples.

This territorial distribution has become so specialised since World War II that specific areas of reference were created: Varese for the helicopters industry, Turin for combat aircraft, Naples for transport aircraft, Genoa and La Spezia for ship building, La Spezia and Brescia for land vehicles and heavy armament, Brescia for light armament, Milan for avionics, Rome and Genoa for naval electronics, Rome for missilery and terrestrial electronics, Florence for electronics applied to land vehicles, Leghorn for the torpedoes industry, Milan and Rome for telecommunications and electronic warfare apparatus. This is only a general picture, that leaves out other smaller production site concentrations, in other areas, to which, anyway, our considerations also apply.

These specialization trends have both favoured the establishment of sub-contractors and part suppliers linked to specific production types and led the training of experts with secondary school and university degrees towards the specializations best suited to the local types of production. Consequently, local universities, national research institutions and local enterprises used to entertain relations and exchange research experience.

This system of interchange is particularly important, because the whole production-training-research system may be endangered in a specific area when a production activity is modified, or even interrupted.

In Italy there has been an interruption of the flow and exchange of personnel and research between universities (mainly Faculties of Engineering) and military enterprises, as a direct consequence of the above phenomenon, which in turn is linked to a specific situation, mentioned below. This interchange was important in Italy, where there are limited possibilities of financing public research directly within enterprises, by leading them towards the civilian sectors relevant to the military industry: new materials, advanced electronics, artificial intelligence, etc.

Furthermore, the financial crisis and the ensuing cuts to public orders prevented Italy from acquiring the professional skills that have become available following the world crisis in the other countries (including the East), therefore there will be a delay in the production of technological innovation in terms of products and processes.

In short, the "Italian pattern" for the acquisition of new technologies has broken up; according to this pattern the interchange between universities and enterprises occurred unofficially: the enterprises employed graduates from the Engineering Faculties, which in turn adapted their curricula and guidelines of research to the needs of armament producers in the military and civilian sectors. This process used to take place informally, without an apparent transfer of financial resources.

From a general point of view, international experience and the existing literature on the issue of restructuring have shown that one of the elements to be taken into account is what could be defined as the degree of "military rigidity" of the individual types of production. Within the military industry the least rigid branch is electronics, followed by ship building, the aeronautical industry, land vehicles, missilery, ammunitions and light and heavy firearms (ordered from the least to the most rigid).

A comparison between the above pattern of the sector and the territorial distribution of production types and their geographical specialization outlines the various problems to be encountered during the rationalization of the Italian military industry, including diversification and conversion. In the same way it is possible to identify the consequences that restructuring will bring about.

Where diversification into the civilian market is relatively easier, on the basis of the above considerations, the local development pattern may be expected to remain effective, requiring adjustment without modification to its inherent structure.

Then there are two problems that must be taken into consideration.

The first problem is the stimulation of public demand for dual products, in that diversification is in any case targeted on the public market (civil defence, management of the territory, purification, health service, etc.). As regards Italy, a difficulty to be solved is that of a sizeable demand, managed by different subjects, often uncoordinated, and poorly standardized. To this end, specific studies and surveys are being developed, under the auspices of the Presidency of the Council of Ministers, to identify relevant solutions, in the framework of the industrial policy and economic planning of the Country.

The second problem is linked to the need to safeguard the planning potential, which is the most important asset of these enterprises. Diversification alone cannot fully replace the lack of good quality activity, arising from investments made by the Defense sector. So far, in Italy almost all military research was financed in the framework of acquisition programmes of the Defense sector itself. At present, on the contrary, it would appear useful to revert the trend and acquire resources to finance military research, regardless of production.

In this way, both civilian and military planning potentials would be maintained, so that enterprises with a low "military rigidity" could be diversified into an integrated production, to meet both military and civilian demand. This course of action has become compulsory, if their survival is to be guaranteed, also on account of the crisis of the above mentioned Italian pattern for the informal interchange between enterprises and universities.

The three year 1994-96 research plan has been drawn up along these guidelines by the Ministry for Universities and Scientific and Technological Research, with a clear practical intent to promote technological innovation, to enable production sectors to rise up to the challenge of competitiveness in a modern economy, in which the limited available resources must be effectively exploited to finance research projects.

In areas where, on the contrary, the specialization of production hinders diversification, the whole pattern of development is bound to break up, so alternative solutions will have to be sought for.

When discussing restructuring, attention focuses exceedingly on plant characteristics and labour specialization, leaving out the characteristics of research activities and of vocational training institutions. On the contrary, the latter must be taken stock of when identifying a new pattern of local development, for two reasons:

1. for their very nature, research and training are more flexible, although they are linked to production, as mentioned above;
2. when acting in a medium term perspective, effective alternative solutions can be conceived on the basis of available qualified labour and research and development potential.

Besides, the problem of possible plant closures must be mitigated by adopting measures in favour of the staff employed at present. However, it must be taken for granted that the youngest part only of personnel can be retrained and employed in production activities that are extremely different from military ones.

Finally, as regards the general process of industrial concentration, now underway in the international military industry, its manifestation in Italy has acquired a specific pattern, also on account of events occurring outside the military market.

These events were the decision to dissolve EFIM, one of the two public corporations in control, among others, of industrial military enterprises, taken on the basis of its financial crisis, and the disengagement from the sector by the only large private group: FIAT.

These events, added to the contemporary drop of internal and international demand, explain why there were no alternatives to the creation of an industrial military aggregate within the FINMECCANICA corporation, whose majority is at present publicly owned. Therefore this industrial aggregate now includes former EFIM companies. For the same reason, FINMECCANICA is now participating in smaller private enterprises and is in control of about 70% of military production.

The process of unification, however, has not improved the organizational effectiveness of enterprises as yet, but rather it brought about the overlapping of leadership, research and development among the various previously independent companies. Consequently the reduction of production was difficult to manage because after the merger, executives were engaged in obtaining the leadership for the personnel of the companies of origin.

This situation practically blocked any form of transfer of executives towards other (civilian and research) sectors, both nationally and abroad. In other words, the effective procedure of redeployment in dual and civilian production sectors of personnel with high technology intensive competence has not been started.

This situation is quite the opposite of what happened in other European Union countries and in the U.S., where, on the contrary, the redeployment of technical executive staff on the market occurred rapidly and, in some cases, satisfactorily (within and outside the country of origin). This difficulty has also adversely affected the flow and interchange of personnel between universities and military enterprises, in the framework of the crisis of the system enterprises-training-research, as was mentioned in the analysis of the territorial situation.

To sum up what has been said so far, in Italy, at present there has been neither a brain drain nor a scientific innovation transfer from the military to the civilian sector, from large public corporations, to private ones, even of small and medium size. What is happening now is the reduction by military enterprises of unqualified labour, while research and development functions are maintained as is technical executive staff, on the assumption that all process potentials can be used in the future and that only production levels are reduced.

However this is only a transition phase, brought about by the restructuring process; in the future a new balanced situation will come about, as a consequence of the completion of corrective interventions, suggested by the analysis of the territorial impact of the military industrial sector.

This new situation will be characterized by a more efficient and effective interchange among universities, research centres and military enterprises; furthermore the "civilian" scientific technological basis will acquire more strategic value than that of the military basis, quite the opposite of what has been the case so far and following the modifications of the economic situation and international politics.